W9-BES-247

The First Twelve Months Of Life

Your Baby's Growth Month by Month

General Editor:

Frank Caplan

Director, The Princeton Center for
Infancy and Early Childhood

BANTAM BOOKS · TORONTO · NEW YORK · LONDON

*This low-priced Bantam Book
has been completely reset in a type face
designed for easy reading, and was printed
from new plates. It contains the complete
text of the original hard-cover edition.*
NOT ONE WORD HAS BEEN OMITTED.

RL8, IL6+

THE FIRST TWELVE MONTHS OF LIFE

*A Bantam Book / published in association with
Grosset & Dunlap, Inc.*

PRINTING HISTORY

*Originally published by Edcom Systems Inc.,
Princeton, N.J. as 12 booklets in 1971 and as
12 booklets in book binder or book box in 1972.*

*Grosset & Dunlap paperback edition published August 1973
20 printings through November 1977*

Grosset & Dunlap hardcover edition published May 1973

2nd printing ...... October 1975	3rd printing .... August 1977

Bantam edition / April 1978

2nd printing .... April 1978	6th printing .... March 1980
3rd printing .... June 1978	7th printing .... April 1980
4th printing .... January 1979	8th printing .... July 1980
5th printing ..... September 1979	9th printing ...... February 1981

ISBN 0-553-20022-4

Published simultaneously in the United States and Canada

---

*Bantam Books are published by Bantam Books, Inc. Its trade-
mark, consisting of the words "Bantam Books" and the por-
trayal of a bantam, is Registered in U.S. Patent and Trademark
Office and in other countries. Marca Registrada. Bantam
Books, Inc., 666 Fifth Avenue, New York, New York 10103.*

PRINTED IN THE UNITED STATES OF AMERICA

18 17 16 15 14 13 12 11 10

Acknowledgments

This book exists only because of the cooperation, encouragement, and information supplied by many researchers working with infants and their mothers, the diligence of a staff who for two full years painstakingly put together these bits and pieces of information into a readable manuscript, and the many professionals who enhanced it with photography, technical editing, and especially their enthusiasm.

We especially wish to thank Dr. T. Berry Brazelton, eminent pediatrician and research fellow at Harvard's Center for Cognitive Studies, who donated time and energy far beyond his assigned task. He assisted our editor with patience and humor, as well as pertinent facts in developing our month-by-month study of infant growth.

Many of the ideas in our book have been inspired by the careful study of Dr. Brazelton's book *Infants and Mothers: Differences in Development.* He is not responsible for any of the ideas or judgments expressed unless directly attributed to him.

We are also grateful to the many professional researchers who allowed our editor to interview them and obtain the most up-to-date research facts. They include Dr. Mary D. Ainsworth, professor of psychology at Johns Hopkins University, Mrs. Franc Balzar, former national director of Parent-Child Centers of the United States Office of Child Development, Dr. Frank Falkner, professor of pediatrics and director of the Fels Research Institute in Cincinnati, Ohio, Dr. Jacob L. Gewirtz, chief of the Section on Early Learning of the National Institute of Mental Health in Bethesda, Maryland, Dr. Eric H. Lenneberg, linguist and professor of psychology and neurobiology at Cornell University in Ithaca, New York, Dr. Michael Lewis, director of the Infant Laboratory at the Educational Testing Service in Princeton, New Jersey, Dr. Lewis P. Lipsitt, research psychologist and director of the Child Study Center at Brown University, Providence, Rhode Island, Dr. Myrtle McGraw, retired professor and director of the Baby Teaching Laboratory at Briarcliff College at Briarcliff Manor, New York, Dr. Frank A. Pederson, research psychologist at the National Institute of Child Health and Human Development in Bethesda, Maryland, and Dr. Roger A. Webb, assistant professor of psychology at the Johns Hopkins University.

We are delighted with the fine, sensitive photographs taken by Ullie Steltzer, as well as the loan of pictures from her personal collection of mothers and babies in other countries.

Our special thanks for the two-year direction of the project by Joan Markessinis Haldas, who acted as chief editor and supervised the researchers assigned to the project. Also to Theresa Caplan for her final technical editing and Dr. Frederic F. Kreisler for his help.

This project would never have been started had we not had the encouragement of parents and some of my former Creative Playthings colleagues who felt that it was necessary to help parents of newborns see that the many "ages and stages" in the life of a young child need sensitive intervention backed up by the latest data on child rearing. Toward this goal of parent education and early environmental stimulation the Princeton Design Center for Infancy and Early Childhood was organized.

My own deep interest in the first three years of life began in 1931, when I was probably the first male nursery school teacher in the United States. During the years 1969 to 1972, our group of researchers has intensively been studying growth and environmental challenges for infants and toddlers and we have developed innovative cribs, play materials, and publications to help children in their earliest years achieve their full potentials.

The years ahead will be exciting ones for new parents. Through the use of new electronic techniques, researchers are finally able to reveal the thinking and maturation processes of infants. Our center hopes to contribute to all advances in parent education and play and learning in infancy.

Frank Caplan

Contents

Introduction

The birth of your baby begins a fascinating year of adventure for you both, a year in which the baby wondrously learns basic rules of physical control, thought, socializing, and communicating. Infancy is a special time in life. A baby is extraordinarily dependent on his parents in comparison to other infant animals. His motor system, especially his hands, is designed with more flexibility than he can possibly control for years. So he must scan his world without physical involvement in it. This imbalance between a baby's senses of sight, hearing, taste, smell, and touch and his virtual physical disability often frustrates the baby and his parents. Luckily he is given enough time to learn the complicated essentials of being human while he is still protected. We hope that *The First Twelve Months of Life* will help you enjoy this challenging time together. As you read each chapter, remember that the first month of life covers the baby's first thirty days, after which he is one month old. The second month of life includes the period from thirty to sixty days. When you finish the twelfth month of life, baby will have reached his first birthday.

In the next twelve months you will see your baby changing faster and working harder than at any other time in his life. He has a lot to learn. In about half that time the little creature you see now will probably begin to sit alone, reach for and grasp a toy, recognize a familiar face, smile, laugh, and hold up his end of a conversation with you by babbling and cooing. By the end of the year, he will stand, probably walk, handle a toy or a spoon, say a few words, and, being a sociable fellow, distinguish the people in his life from the strangers, and form strong attachments to some of them. He will even have settled down to a routine of three meals a day, an afternoon nap, and sleeping through the night. He will have learned that something heard is something to see, that things seen may be grasped, and that things grasped have permanence even when out of hand and sight. He will have begun to understand what part of the world is "him" and what part is not, and how to influence both parts.

How is all this accomplished? To some extent it is a natural process of unfolding with the same sequence of stages occurring in all babies everywhere. Development follows a head-down-to-toes direction. Eye muscles come under control first, then the facial muscles and neck, and finally the trunk and the legs. Development also follows a center-outward-to-fingertips direction. At one stage the baby will wave his arms, use them to help him to sit, and reach for toys hung over his crib. At a later stage, he will control his wrist, fingers, and thumb so that he can pick up and release things precisely.

There are variations though in the time at which these stages occur. Not all babies sit, smile, or reach out at exactly the same age. Do not expect your baby to conform to any schedule of development. Keep in mind that every baby develops at his own rate with his own style, and each is an individual. A baby's drive toward motor achievements can push him months ahead of other babies and frighten an insecure mother. Yet such precocity can and does exist in other babies too. That is why the infant statistical model is not an inviolable god of authority. A baby is born into this world with basic drives. He wants to survive and he wants to fit into and "please" his environment. Yet even a young infant actively seeks stimulation. Far from being passive, a baby strives to master his environment, as well as identify with it. What happens to these drives is a product of the exchange between a baby's unique heredity and his world.

From the very moment of birth, individual differences are apparent and begin to determine your reaction to your new infant. Babies can be individual enough to want to practice their budding talents alone sometimes. Not only do they not need mother or father around at times, they do not want them. On the other hand, your baby may seem to want constant cuddling. In the early weeks these differences are less obvious than the similarity of a baby's needs and his responses when needs are or are not met. His needs and growth will be less similar later when customs, culture, and even social class are more significant. Even so, early and very real differences can be very exciting to the baby and to the mother and father who recognize them. Enjoy the time you spend with him and respect him as the person he is. With this in mind, you need not feel guilty when you come into conflict with your new and precious but not always helpless infant.

Because you and your new baby are unique, you must find your own way with your own very special baby. Science cannot make the same specific recommendations to millions of people because each baby develops in a different environment. People in totally different cultures cannot be advised to feed or train their children in the same way, just as American parents cannot be told to discipline their babies identically. Each family's personalities and home are unique. You and your husband are the most critical influences in your infant's first year of life. If we may cite just one small example, your infant's ability to demand and get a response from the environment is first experienced in relation to you. Before a child will work to master his environment, he has to feel that a loved one in it is going to respond to him. The quality of mothering and the interaction between mother and baby in the earliest weeks substantially determine whether development in the first year will continue. No child is doomed by birth to neurosis if his environment allows him to develop to his fullest intellectual potential and provides a happy, stimulating and healthy childhood in which the capacity to love and to be loved is rewardingly learned through his earliest experiences with his parents. Our parents used to be told not to pick up an infant or cuddle him and that too much handling would "spoil" him. Now we realize that when a parent enjoys playing with his baby it not only gives the baby pleasure, it sets a precedent for his getting pleasure from relationships with other people.

There are no strict rules. Your individual reactions, instinct, and intuition may be as right as the idealized suggestions of an "authority" may be wrong. Each baby becomes a special experience for a mother. Young parents do better to chart their own behavior from the cues set out for them by their own baby as well as from "models" in infant literature. The broad outlines of growth and developments are universal, but the details have to be inscribed for each baby by parents who are responsive to his particular needs at each stage of his life.

Once young parents recognize the wide world of normal infant behavior, they will better understand the how and why of each step in development that this book describes. It helps to know that baby's state—whether he is crying, drowsy, active, or alert—influences his responses in those troublesome first three months far more than it does later. Or that a baby cries not because he is angry at mother, but because he is frustrated with his inability to grapple with a world he is becoming aware of. A mother in the United States today almost has to know more. Without the guidance and diversion of the grandparents, aunts, and cousins of yesterday's extended family, she is alone with her baby for long stretches of time. Her only outlet may be enjoying him—a delight that comes from confident understanding and learning from him.

This book will bring you information about how all children mature. Each chapter will discuss infant development appropriate to each month, pinpointing motor, language, mental, and social abilities.

Besides stressing the role and value of parent-child interaction and the importance and influence of environment, each chapter features a special event most likely to appear in that or neighboring months, even though the topic may be touched on elsewhere. The only aspect of caretaking we are including is feeding because mother spends a great deal of her time doing it and what she does in feeding ties in very tightly to her other behavior toward her baby.

We have not portrayed an "average" mean because the averages were computed several decades ago. We have also tried to acquaint you with the vast individual differences among normal babies. Because the human infant is so changeable and "unknown," we have gleaned information from books, articles, monographs, research reports, and professional papers.

Infant research is exciting, informative, challenging, and exacting. It is still new, however, and its research tools are tentative. The strict model of laboratory settings based on structured, inflexible test situations blurs the child's vital individuality. Therefore we have chosen to mellow the book with the seasoned, long-term observations of outstanding scientists and pediatricians, among them Dr. T. Berry Brazelton of Harvard's Center for Cognitive Studies.

This book describes a sequence, not a timetable. Within that general framework, you and your baby will have to discover what is right for him. We say first month for convenience, but do not go by the calendar. It may last a longer or shorter time for your particular baby.

A word about gender. Writers on child care may some day succeed in introducing into the language a word that means both "he" and "she." Meantime we will use the convention of the masculine pronoun, but we assure you that unless we are talking about something where sex makes a difference, everything we say about "him" refers to your new daughter as well. Similarly, until the English language invents a popular term for brother and sister, you may occasionally find the word "sib," a borrowing from social science literature that means either.

We hope you fathers will read this book along with your wives. Your role, possibly more important behind the scenes in the first year, is critical to your family in ways we hope to explain. The role of firm decisiveness and strong, loving support, for example, may have been a major lack in the fathering for our generation. Mother and father should decide together about what to do with the baby.

Whether you are new parents or "old hands," we would like to give you both a feeling for the infant and his world that will help you experience and enjoy it together. At the same time, we hope we can help you feel less hesitant and more sure of yourselves as mothers and fathers than our parents' generation. Parents who give of themselves and respect their children as individuals, yet can say "no" as well as "yes," can confidently let go of them at the right time. In the meantime, we want to assist you in choosing a personal style of living and learning with your baby by offering you the wide spectrum of normal and expected infant behaviors and infant rearing practices.

THE
FIRST
WEEK

The Newborn

THE FIRST WEEK
The Newborn

A mother-in-waiting often imagines her first baby to be like the delightful three- or four-month-olds she has been looking at all her life in picture books. She soon discovers at birth or the first feeding that nothing could be farther from the truth. But balancing this rude awakening is a marvelous discovery—her baby is neither the helpless nor the unindividualized human neophyte he was once "scientifically" described to be.

Delivery is as difficult for the baby as it is for the mother. It is a battle lasting anywhere from four to twenty-four hours, from which the new arrival emerges splattered with his mother's blood and a thick, greasy, white material called vernix, which lets him slip through the birth canal.

He is no beauty. His skin may be discolored. The skin itself is wrinkled and loose and often ready to scale in creased places, such as hands and feet. Some newborns have extra stores of flesh, part of which is fluid, that make them look fat. The condition helps to tide the infant over until he can eat. As the extra padding disappears during the first week, it leaves the skin peeled and cracked, as the photograph on page 20 shows.

Besides the hair on his head, dark, fine hair called "lanugo" may cover the newborn's body. This hair matted with vernix gives him a strange pasted look. Even his cheeks, ears, shoulders, and back may be furry. Lanugo, a leftover from our monkey ancestors, disappears at the latest about the fourth month of life, leaving the baby soft and smooth.

The newborn's head is also not the most attractive in the world. It may be swollen at the top because of pressure against the pelvic outlet during the last hours of labor, and it is often molded like a melon with a point at the back. However, since mother's pelvis is usually an inch narrower than the circumference of her baby's head, this molding is quite useful. It allows the skull bones to overlap, with no damage to the brain, so the fetus' head can emerge from the mother successfully.

Generally the newborn's physical description reads like a prizefighter's. His face may be puffy and bluish; his ears may be pressed to his head in bizarre positions—for example, matted forward on his cheeks; his nose, flattened and skewed to one side by the squeeze through the pelvis; his eyes puffy; his eyelids swollen; and his temples and cheeks temporarily bruised if the obstetrician has used forceps.

Bowlegs from his position in the womb are usual, and his feet may look "wind-blown" or be cocked pigeon-toed from being up beside his head for so long. They can be flexed and put in a normal position at birth.

As if this struggle were not enough, the battered arrival must, for his very life, be manhandled further. The obstetrician cuts the umbilical cord and sucks the newborn's airways with a bulb-suction. From then on, the baby's head is kept down. Even though it appears unnecessary for babies who cry and breathe readily upon delivery, this suction is vital. Otherwise the first breath may draw fluid and mucus further into the lungs, making the baby gag, his breathing slow, and his temperature drop. The baby's first gasping cry, which the obstetrician may encourage with the classic slap, is also vital. It fills the baby's lungs with air and changes him from a parasite living off the oxygen in his mother's blood to an independent organism with his own circulatory system. As he begins to breath, his color improves. Bursts of rapid, increasingly deeper breaths follow long periods of gasps, chokes, sneezes, and no perceptible breathing. While his breathing patterns are frightening to an inexperienced listener like his new mother, they are perfectly normal to the professional. Wrapped in several sheets to keep him warm, the neonate is wheeled from the delivery room, and the obstetrician turns to the mother.

How stunning it must be to be thrust suddenly into a new, bright, airy world so totally different from the dark, moist warmth of the womb. Despite the drama of human birth, newborns who have had a comfortable stay in the womb and are born when due can withstand even more than the usual trauma of birth. And nature allows them, unlike their mothers, a deep nourishing sleep after the contest. In the nursery, nurses rinse the blood and vernix from the infant, wash him with special medicated soap to avoid infection, and inject him with Vitamin K to prevent internal bleeding. The infant, diapered and dressed, is tilted head down in his crib. Curled in his familiar fetal position, he relaxes and falls into a deep, comalike sleep. Only the most active infants ever interrupt this. Lusty crying is very rare. Most newborns just startle, jerk briefly, or gag up mucus irregularly. Only vigorous outside stimulation disturbs them. A brief change in breathing, for example, is the only almost imperceptible response to loud noise.

In these first few days, the infant recovers from his mother's labor, the delivery, and the new stresses of the world outside the womb. Although physiologically ready to function, the infant has to stabilize his circulatory, breathing, digestion, elimination, body temperature, and hormone mechanisms, which also must start working faster for his new and independent life. Suppose *you* had been stuck in a damp sack about twenty-one inches long and a foot or so wide, in which you could hardly move and barely hear, and had no chance to breathe, smell, taste, or see anything? Then in a split second *you* have to get rid of the wastes that someone else had been relieving you of. You have to breathe for yourself in a strange world that can be cold, hot, dry, or damp. You are expected to see and to hear and can suddenly smell strange things, called odors. No wonder a baby cries when he sees his first light!

The baby's self-reorganizing leaves him little energy for eating and digesting. Many babies show this effort by actual resistance to being roused to eat. During his first days a baby is often unprepared to digest even milk, which he occasionally gags up with mucus. His stores of extra sugar, fat, tissues, and fluid sustain him until his mother's milk comes in, usually about three days or so after his delivery.

Meantime, mother herself is recovering, but she has time to think and to worry as she lies alone in her hospital bed. New mothers wonder if the baby is *really* theirs, repeatedly ask doctors and nurses for assurance that the baby is all right, worry if the baby cries too much or too little, and are often shocked by their baby's appearance. Their first response to the offspring placed in their arms is just as likely to be "My God, did I really do this?" as love at first sight.

Two of the new mother's most common concerns, pediatricians report, are about the effects of medication on the baby and the ability of the mother to nurse her infant. A woman's medication during labor, sometimes entirely necessary, does affect her infant. The effects are temporary, however. By and large, the newborn can still appear wide awake at delivery!

New mothers also wonder whether they will ever feel positively toward their new baby or whether they will be mother enough for him and the other children awaiting them at home. They may resent relinquishing the balance established with a first baby, doubt the new child's ability to adjust to a brother or sister, as well as their ability to help him do this. Many feel so confused they dare not express these feelings even to themselves. Yet such conflict is natural. Giving up independence to become a mother is never easy. Dr. Brazelton writes, "The balance a new mother has achieved as a woman and wife is shaken, especially if she has been married only a year or so. She must face a new and demanding role—that of having an unknown human being completely dependent on her. Any woman who really cares how she meets these responsibilities may well wonder whether she will ever be equal to them."

Many hospital staffs do little to allay a new mother's fears. Frequently they unconsciously increase them. When a mother seeks help she is often quieted with stereotyped reassurances or condescension, even though reassurance about the normalcy of her baby can be so easy. Tests are made at birth to assess whether a baby's reflexes and general physical condition are normal. A serious discussion with a doctor allows the mother to express her fears—therapeutic in itself—and permits the doctor to understand and explain them to her. Often the new mother, already coping with feelings of inadequacy, must listen to reports of others' efficiency. The inference in a nurse's classic comment—he's so quiet and good in the nursery—hardly helps a mother trying desperately to rouse her baby to nurse. But one reason the baby is being difficult is that he is having a hard time. Remember that he is being asked to start adjusting immediately to totally new, very definite adult patterns of feeding and resting.

Yet mothering, even in the hospital where your baby is away from you so often, can be fun. By the third or fourth day, when you and your baby have recovered a little from his dramatic entrance, you even may be able to enjoy him. Holding a little baby is lovely. Feeding periods are your chance to exercise your maternal feelings—to play, cuddle, and communicate with your baby and to begin to know him. You may find that even this early you can calm his crying or help him quiet himself with crooning or a gently placed hand. When your baby is upset, you can be an ally instead of a contestant in his struggle to feed well. Vigorous squirming may mean independence and physical sturdiness, not opposition to you. Quietness may signal resting, not disinterest.

You may even begin speculating about your infant's future coloring. Its best predictor is your own and your husband's coloring. There aren't too many other clues you can go on now. Many babies have "mongolian spots," so-called because the Mongolian races usually have them, as do Negroes and brunette Caucasians. These clusters of dark pigment about the base of the baby's spine diffuse eventually and the "spots" disappear over time. Hair color is unreliable. A baby's hair falls out and is replaced by permanent hair around his fourth or fifth month. His new hair color can be dramatically different. Eye color, too, can change any time in the first year. Most Caucasian babies are born with "blue" eyes, but a few are born with brown. Black babies have colorless eyes. In most dark-complexioned Caucasians, the muddying of the iris, the colored area around the pupil, occurs in the first few weeks. Usually by six months you can predict brown by the muddy look. Eyes that will be blue stay clear blue.

Tone color of the skin is only a fair clue to your baby's future coloring. Most babies undergo color changes during their first week of life. From birthday purple, they gradually change to pinkish purple, to cherry red, to yellow, all of which reflect changes in the circulatory system.

Around the third day, your baby's skin and eyes may look slightly yellow or tanned as if he had been sunning himself. Decomposing red blood cells, extras needed for the womb's lower oxygen supply in comparison to the outside air, cause this perfectly normal third-to-fifth-day jaundice. The breakdown, coupled with mild dehydration, yields a chemical called bilirubin, which the infant's immature liver just cannot get rid of. As the baby absorbs milk and his cells rehydrate, the jaundice washes out.

You will also find that your baby will eventually attain the balance he has worked so hard for. The weight he may have lost by the third day in comparison to his birthweight is all but regained, thanks to your feeding. The umbilical cord is still there but drying. He is losing his jaundiced look, his color is improving, and although the skin on his hands and feet may be cracked and peeling, he looks filled out.

Infant Power: What He Can Do With His Body

Besides these visible improvements, newborns are just not as helpless as they look. First of all, the activities needed to sustain life function at birth. A newborn can breathe, suck, swallow, and get rid of wastes. He can look, hear, taste, smell, feel, turn his head, and signal for help from the first minute. Right from the start, a baby's attention can be captured by sharply contoured or circular shapes. This indicates your newborn's mental curiosity is not entirely swamped by his needs for food and comfort.

Physically, newborns are admittedly limited. A newborn is tiny. From head to heels, he may be about twenty-one inches long and weighs seven and one-half pounds. His head, about fourteen inches long, is almost two thirds of his height and an inch bigger than his chest, so he is understandably awkward. Just try to imagine yourself in his shape. Even with your maturity and skill you would have a hard time getting around if your head were twice as big and your arms and legs half their size. He is bound by where you put him, and he is at the mercy of his bodily needs. His heart beats twice as fast as a grownup's, 120 beats a minute, and he breathes twice as fast as you do, about thirty-three times a minute. He may urinate as many as eighteen times and move his bowels from four to seven times in twenty-four hours. He sleeps fourteen to eighteen hours of his twenty-four-hour day. On the average, he is alert and comfortable for only thirty minutes in a four-hour period.

Reflexes govern his movements, which are automatic and beyond his control. For example, if you stroke your newborn's hand or foot on the back or top, the whole arm or leg withdraws slightly and the hand or foot flexes and then returns so that fingers or toes may grasp your finger. This withdrawal reflex only exists until the baby begins to use his limbs in a different way—legs for standing and stepping, arms for reaching.

There are many other reflexes your newborn will show you. If you hold him in a standing position and gently press the sole of one foot and then the other to the bed, he will draw up each leg successively as if walking. Without helping it, your newborn can actually "walk" across a bed. Almost a year after the newborn's walk reflex vanishes, it reappears as the voluntary, complex art of walking.

One of the most frequent and dramatic reflexes of the newborn is the Moro reflex, a vestige from our ape ancestry. If the baby is handled roughly, hears a very loud noise, sees a bright light, or feels a sudden change in position, he startles, arches his back, and throws his head back. At the same time, he flings out his arms and legs, then rapidly closes them to the center of his body, and flexes it as if he were falling. As he cries, he startles, then cries because of the startle. This reflex, normal in all newborns, tends to disappear at three to four months of age. Steady pressure on any part of his body will calm him. If you hold his arm firmly flexed at his shoulder, he will quiet even though undressed and free of restraints.

Try stroking different parts of your infant's body. If you stroke the palm of his hand or the sole of his foot at the base of the toes, he will grasp your finger. The more premature he is, the more tenacious his grasp. By using his toe grasp, you can lift your baby's leg off a mattress. With his hand grasp, you can gently pull him to a sitting position or even suspend him in the air hanging onto your fingers for dear life, as if to a tree branch. (Better leave this one to the experts.) Stroking the outside of the infant's sole sets off an opposite reflex, called the Babinski. The toes spread and the big toe shoots up in the air.

As you will learn as soon as you start feeding your baby, stroking his cheek or around his mouth makes him root or turn toward the stroking object. This rooting reflex helps him find the breast, and the sucking reflex follows. Touching the inside of his mouth, which is more sensitive than the surrounding area, stimulates this reflex most. A bottle is thus easier to suck than the breast because the bottle touches this area.

Dr. Lewis P. Lipsitt of Brown University believes that babies have definite taste preferences at birth; they suck sweeter solutions faster and spit out sour ones.

If you stroke your newborn's cheek or palm—extremes of

a hand-to-mouth continuum—you will start another reflex. The infant's mouth will root, his arm will flex, and his hand will come up to his open mouth. A newborn often sucks on his fist noisily for long periods (fifteen minutes or so), and so energetically that his whole body tenses and changes color until he loses his fist and random activity takes over. You need do little to start this hand-to-mouth cycle. Hand-to-mouth activity and finger sucking are probably common in the womb. In fact, pediatricians and obstetricians have seen these right after delivery. A premature newborn struggling to survive can actually clear his air passage by sucking on his fist and swallowing the mucus that chokes him.

Most of the newborn's remaining physical abilities are quite limited. His preferred lying-down positions vary between a rag-doll frog-leg and half-extended arms to a fetal compression with all limbs pulled in. Twitches, jerky startles, and convulsive movements are the order of the day. In fact the difference between the movements of premature and full-term infants shows the importance of time and learning. The preemie's jerky flailing of limbs precedes the smooth, freely cycling, self-controlled arcs of movement of a full-term baby, who less frequently displays the preemie's movements. In contrast to slow, easy, coordinated movements of the arms, legs, and head, the baby rapidly thrusts arms and legs that suddenly flex and return to his torso.

In general, the baby's responses are less specific than they will be when his nervous system is more mature. He may have the same response, such as sucking, to very different things—a light, a doorbell, or a sudden draft. He may also react with his whole body when he feels sudden changes in temperature, pressure, light, and sound.

Yet the newborn is not impotent, as the government-sponsored research of scientists like Robert L. Fantz at Western Reserve University, William Kessen of Yale, Peter Wolff of the Massachusetts Institute of Technology, and Burton White and Jerome S. Bruner of Harvard shows.

Says Dr. Frantz, "The findings to date have tended to destroy the myth that the world of the newborn is a big blooming confusion, that his visual field is a formless blur, that his mind is a blank slate. . . . The infant sees a patterned and organized world which he explores discriminatingly with the limited means at his command."

Speaking of what he called "the new look in research on

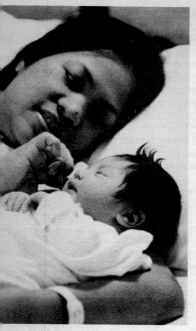
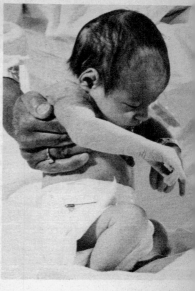

infancy," Dr. L. Joseph Stone of the Department of Child Study at Vassar says, "Our conception of the newborn is changing; the neonate is more sensitive to and aware of the world, he is more responsive to it, and he is earlier influenced by his interaction with it than we had previously believed. Even his reflexes are far from the purposeless activities they were once thought to be."

The newborn can already protect himself. For several days after birth, his gag reflex helps him spit up the mucus from his mother's womb so that he can breathe. A strong blink reflex protects his eyes from too much light. If one part of his body is exposed to a sharp temperature change, his whole body changes color and temperature, he pulls in his limbs to reduce the exposed body surface, and finally begins to cry and shiver to try to improve his body's circulation and to protest this unwelcome change. As soon as he is covered and warm, he will quiet.

He can avoid smothering. If you place an object over his nose and mouth, he will mouth it vigorously and then twist his head violently from side to side. If these maneuvers fail to remove it, he will cross each arm over his face to try to knock the object off.

On his tummy, he will lift his head from the bed and turn it to one side. Place your hand against his foot and he will crawl forward, arch his body, and even raise himself on his arms. Sometimes newborns flip themselves completely over. At this stage they are unaware of propelling themselves across space, but around the seventh month they will know what they are doing.

A newborn also tries to right himself. You will see one of your baby's righting reflexes if you pull him by his arms from his back to a sitting position. His eyes will open wide like a china doll's and his whole shoulder area will tense as he helps to pull up his head. As long as you pull your baby to sit slowly and steadily, the wobbling of his neck won't hurt him. Once seated, he will try to keep his oversized head upright. As his head flops forward, he will try to keep it in line, but it will "overshoot" and fall backward. As he tries again, it will tilt forward. These valiant efforts are righting reflexes. In just four months time he will be able to hold his head upright.

The newborn can also avoid pain. If you hurt any part of him, he will withdraw from you if he can. Stroking one leg will make the other cross and push your hand away. If you poke the upper part of his body, his hand comes over to grasp yours. Then he will try to push or bat you away.

Dr. Brazelton reports that when he has to take blood from an infant's heel, "The infant will pull his foot away. When this doesn't work, the other foot comes over persistently to push."

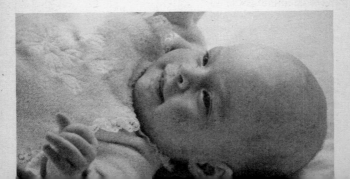

These reflexes are not just immediately useful. Your baby's brain stores and learns from all these reflex experiences, building for the future. The baby's righting reflexes probably contribute to the development of his concepts of space. For several months, the tonic neck reflex helps him learn to use each side of his body separately and to watch and use his hands *voluntarily*. If you or the baby turn his head to one side, the arm on the side to which his head is turned extends, the knee on that side flexes, and the opposite arm crooks like a fencer's.

Some reflexes, such as coughs, sneezes, and yawns, never go away completely, and traces of reflexes like the tonic neck reflex and the Moro reflex show up in adult sleep positions and in our responses to being startled. Newborns also swim reflexively. Like any amphibian, an infant can rhythmically extend and flex his arms and legs, swing his trunk from side to side, and stop breathing for short periods under water. Newborns rarely choke or breathe in water because their gag reflexes are still too strong. About a year later, swimming movements will reappear and signal an opportune time to teach your toddler to swim.

Sense Perception

Even more exciting, your baby is a thinking, feeling being. True, his brain is still immature and he remembers objects only if they reappear within two and one-half seconds; otherwise they are new as far as he is concerned. So far satisfaction and displeasure are the only emotions researchers and mothers have clearly discerned. But your baby *does* learn. He learns to distinguish the nipple from the surrounding skin or bottle. He also seems able to distinguish people from objects. Researchers at Harvard's Center for Cognitive Studies write, "From the first week there seem to be features that characterize orientation to a small object . . . within six to seven inches from the eyes which are different from the features that characterize responses to people."

The newborn learns to expect food at a certain time and protests any change in service. Researchers' observations of three groups of infants two to eight days old showed their activity dropped sharply after nursing. Changing one group from a three-hour to a four-hour schedule made them much

more active and fussy in the fourth hour than babies who
had to cope with only one schedule for eight days.

Your newborn can focus his attention on a particular new
thing he sees or hears—amidst a bombardment of stimulation. Doing so quiets him. He can prefer one reaction to
another (at a particular moment), and can tune in or out
when stimulation is appropriate or inappropriate to his
particular state at that moment, or to his general stage of
development. He can choose what he needs from his environment, as long as you give him something to choose from. He
can suppress many potentially harmful reactions. In fact, a
barrage of strong or changing events can put a newborn to
sleep. An infant being given a cardiogram and brainwave test
can cry with discomfort for a few seconds if rubber bands
around his scalp are too tight. Then he may quiet abruptly
and remain motionless throughout testing, seemingly asleep
except that his arms and legs are pulled tightly into the
fetal "ball." Bright lights and sharp noises barely seem to
disturb him and his brainwave shows the pattern of sleep. As
soon as the stimulation stops and the tight bands are off,
however, he cries lustily.

The newborn's most impressive powers are sensory. Your
baby can feel changes in temperature, distinguish tastes, and
by the third or fourth day show preference for sweet and
dislike of bitter flavors. Dr. Lewis P. Lipsitt of Brown University has shown that newborns not only can distinguish between two smells, they actually despise foul odors. In a series
of experiments he discovered some amazing facts. Babies
with as little as fifty-five hours of experience on earth can
differentiate smells—and with no practice. When introduced
to strong (irritating to adult) odors, babies become startled
and very active. They will turn their heads away and cry. As
they grow older, their heartbeats slow down, showing that
babies get bored with the odor game or even get used to the
tense odors if provided in small doses.

They are also very sensitive to touch and pressure. Touch
is almost a language for infants. Skin contact and warmth,
especially from mother's body, are probably the most potent
stimulation for infants in the first few months of life. Like a
radar screen picking up vibrations, your baby soaks in your
feelings about him from your handling. He can sense rough,
inappropriate, or insufficient handling, and he appreciates
touch suited to his style. In fact, touch is so important that

infants with caretakers who give them adequate physical stimulation and little else progress well for the first five or six months. As the late Dr. Lawrence K. Frank indicated, "One of the major reasons for defective development in institutional babies is the infrequent handling they receive." Many fussing or crying babies will quiet and become alert and interested when a hand is placed on their tummies or a foot is firmly restrained. Swaddling may be even more effective because it combines the quieting, soothing aspect of touch with firm, steady pressure.

Babies are also born hearing. Tests show that newborns blink, jerk, and draw in their breath sharply in response to sounds. They also prefer certain sounds to others. Many mothers report that music, the hum of motors, soft rhythmic drumming, and human voices calm fussy, irritable babies.

A newborn distinguishes volume. Even in the delivery room, he can startle or shudder at a loud noise, then shut it out the second or third time around. Soft noises, like crooning, produce fleeting, crooked smiles. The newborn can also localize a sound ten minutes after birth. He will become alert with a start, control his startle reaction, and turn to the sound, sometimes shifting his attention and energy completely away from an important function such as sucking. Length of a sound also affects him. He will respond to a ten-second tone but not one lasting one or two seconds. He distinguishes pitch. Research indicates that newborns, before learning can be a factor, quiet and become alert more consistently in response to a high-pitched than a low voice—possibly in readiness for mother's rather than father's voice.

One of the most exciting discoveries of the growth sciences has been that young infants are visually sophisticated organisms. Newborns see. A newborn will alert, frown, and gradually try to focus on a red or soft yellow object dangled about eight to twelve inches before him. Beyond that range, he probably has only a hazy image and his eyes may wander independently or flair outward for awhile. Once he gets his eyes together, he will stare intently at an object, eyes glistening. His face will brighten and his body quiet. He will follow or track the object with his eyes and turn his head slowly and jerkily when the object is moved slowly from side to side. He can even follow it up and down if it moves very slowly. This visual responsiveness is evident even in the delivery room. Since his experience with vision has been zero in the womb, you know he is born seeing. In fact, some newborns delight so much in seeing, they will actually drop the nipple and turn to an attractive object.

The newborn is also sensitive to other visual matters, such as the intensity of light. He will shut his eyes tightly and keep them shut after being exposed to a bright white light. He will squint if the light in a room changes.

He can discriminate shapes and patterns (the arrangements of lines and details) from birth. He prefers patterns to dull or bright solid colors and looks longer at stripes and angles than at circular patterns. Within three weeks, however, his preference shifts dramatically to the human face. Why should a baby with so little visual experience attend more to a human face than to any other kind of pattern? Some scientists think this preference represents a built-in advantage for the human species. The object of prime importance to the physically helpless infant is a human being. Babies seem to have an inborn tendency to perceive the human face as potentially rewarding. Researchers also point out that the newborn wisely relies more on pattern than on outline, size, or color. Pattern remains stable, while outline changes with point of view; size, with distance from an object; and brightness and color, with lighting. Facial pattern is probably the most reliable way to identify people under different circumstances, and the best way to judge their reactions and attitudes is by the details of their facial expression. This "imprinting" of the human face is an important basis for all subsequent learning and for the growth of attachment and love.

Mothers have always claimed that they could see their newborns looking at them as they held them, in spite of what they have been told. The experts who thought that perception had to await physical development and the consequence of action were wrong for several reasons. Earlier research techniques were less sophisticated than they are today. Physical skills were once used to indicate perception of objects—skills like visual tracking and reaching for an object, both of which the newborn does poorly. Then, too, assumptions that the newborn's eye and brain were too immature for anything as sophisticated as pattern recognition caused opposing data to be discarded or misinterpreted. Since perception of form was widely believed to follow perception of more "basic" qualities such as color and brightness, the possibility of its presence from birth was discounted out of hand.

How *your* baby responds to sights, sounds, and touch depends on their intensity, his length of exposure to them, and also his state at the time. Sudden jarring will cause a startle, but rhythmic rocking soothes. When hungry or sleepy, he is less aware of sensations from the outside world than in moments of quiet but alert wakefulness, when he feels no discomfort from within.

One of a Kind

Newborns are more powerful socially than previously believed. Your newborn is unaware that he exists. But he *is* an individual—with all the potential for impact that a real personality has on another human being. Every newborn varies infinitely from every other—in looks, feelings, movements, reactions to stimulation, and in his effect on his mother.

Babies are different even before their arrival. Some lie quietly in the womb, others allow their mothers little sleep in the last months before delivery. They "wake up" as mother prepares for bed and bicycle or kick for hours. Some infants are delivered from the womb screaming and fighting. Others appear sluggishly. Some newborns stay awake for as long as an hour and a half after birth before their first sleep. Others will fall into their deep sleep within a quarter of an hour after delivery. Boys in general differ from girls. They are more active, stronger, and less sensitive to pain.

Some newborns suck better than others. Some are alert longer and more frequently. Some prefer visual stimulation, others auditory. Some handle several kinds of stimulation simultaneously, others cannot. Some are more influenced by their needs for sleep, food, or physical comfort than others. Some are hard to arouse from deep sleep. Others will shoot directly from sleep to an inaccessible state of intense squalling. Some babies respond more vigorously than others to stimulation of all kinds. Some kick and flail as they become excited while others become muscularly rigid. Some are "criers" right from the first day.

Many newborns can be soothed easily. Quieting others demands vigor. Some cannot be calmed with crooning, quiet rocking, or cuddling, or with a bottle or the breast alone. Tight swaddling, plus vigorous rocking, plus a bottle or the breast may do the trick. Do not feel awkward and unhappy if you have to quiet your baby this way. It may be the only thing that works. Many babies often behave like this and most do at certain times of the day. As Birns, Blank, and Bridger, researchers at Yeshiva University in New York City, have pointed out, the mother's competence in protecting her baby from undue stress is what is important, not her way of doing it.

Other babies are so quiet and peaceful that new mothers may worry about whether they are normal. They cry rarely, their color deepens slightly, and generally they respond almost imperceptibly to stimulation. They express disturbance subtly—a frown, a whimper, or sucking a finger or two. They may be limp and inactive for long periods. In contrast to a very active newborn who chokes down his formula with greedy, noisy gulps and then spits up some of it, this kind of baby feeds calmly and efficiently, bubbles quickly, and returns promptly to rest. Such neonates are not necessarily quiet because of the influence of their mother's sedation during delivery. They are quiet because it is part of their personality.

Scientists are already conjecturing on the implications of these differences that appear at birth. A baby who cries no matter how hard you try to calm him may evoke very different motherly feelings than one who quiets within moments of soothing. Babies who respond to sights rather than sounds may fear strangers earlier and more severely. Newborns who are less affected by their internal needs may, as adults, be less hampered by their moods in working, thinking, and socializing. Newborns who rocket from one state to another without spending much time in between may convey their needs more clearly to their parents.

The reasons for newborn differences are a little clearer. Each baby starts life with a unique set of inherited characteristics—from each parent and from their families before them. Then, too, mother's diet, medication, personal habits, and general emotional health affect her newborn. So does the birth experience itself—the length of labor and type of delivery.

Besides, newborns are not really all the same age at birth. Age is counted from birth, but some babies have more developmental time in the womb than others. Premature babies may miss out on whole months of prenatal growth, and even some "full-term" babies are born a week or two before their due date. Others do not put in an appearance for as much as a week or two after they are expected. The baby lying next to yours in the hospital nursery and born on the same date as he was may thus be weeks older or younger. An "older" newborn is likely to be better developed, stronger, able to suck more vigorously, and less easily upset by sudden noises.

Whatever the implications or the causes of "difference," you can see from such variation that any description of the "normal" infant describes a statistical average, not any one baby. You should not expect such a profile to resemble your baby in all particulars. What it *can* do is give you some insight into the process of your baby's development—the way in which one kind of behavior leads to the next. The best way to understand your baby is to study the baby himself, learn his "cues," and respond to them appropriately. It is the little ways in which he differs from all others that make him a special, interesting individual—*your* baby.

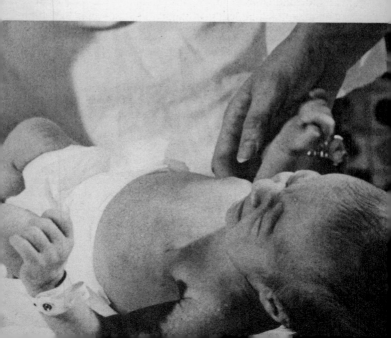

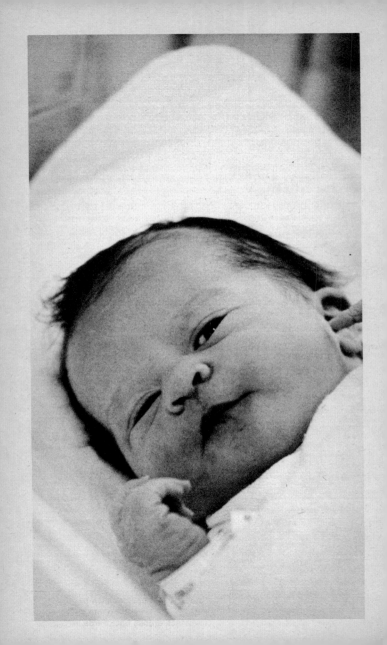

The Newborn's Reflexes

If you	Then the baby's
Tap bridge of the nose, or shine a bright light suddenly into the eyes, clap hands about eighteen inches from infant's head, or touch white of eye with cotton	Eyes close tightly.
Make sudden contact or noise	Head drops backward, neck extends, arms and legs fling outward and back sharply (Moro reflex).
Extend forearms at elbow	Arms flex briskly.
Lightly prick soles of feet	Knee and foot flex.
Stand infant; press foot to bed	Feet step.
Pull baby to sit	Eyes snap open, shoulders tense. Baby tries unsuccessfully to right head (China doll reflex).
Put baby on tummy on flat surface	Head turns to side and lifts. Baby crawls, lifts self with arms.
Support chest on water surface	Arms and legs "swim."
Place on back and turn head to side	Body arches away from face side; arm on face side extends, leg draws up; other arm flexes (tonic neck reflex).
Stroke foot or hand on top	Limb withdraws, arches, returns to grasp.
Stroke palm or sole at base of digits	Limb grasps.
Stroke outside of sole	Toes spread, large toe sticks up.
Tap upper lips sharply	Lips protrude.
Stroke cheek or mouth	Mouth roots, head turns and tongue moves toward stroking object; mouth sucks.
Stroke cheek or palm	Mouth roots; arm flexes; hand goes to open mouth.
Place object over nose and mouth	Mouth works vigorously; head twists, arms fling across face.
Stroke leg, upper part of body	Opposite leg or hand crosses to push your hand away; withdraws.
Rotate baby to side	Head turns, eyes precede direction of rotation.
Suspend by legs	Body curls to upside-down ball, legs extend, arms drop into straight line; neck arches backwards.

Motor

Large

Reflexes control arm, leg, and hand movements.
Nonreflexive activity is gross and random. Wiggles, kicks, flings arms and legs in all directions, twitches convulsively.

Responds with total body to sudden changes.

Moves head side to side, possibly up and down.

When held on adult's shoulder, lifts head and adjusts posture.

On tummy, lies in floppy, froglike position or rolled into ball.

Sitting

Head falls backward or forward when pulled to sitting position.

Small

Hands fisted. Reflex grasp.
Reflex swallow.
Eyes flair outward.

Language

Active

Sounds are animal-like.

Cries.

Please do not regard this chart as a rigid timetable. Babies are unpredictable. Some perform an activity earlier or later than the chart indicates.

Growth Chart

Mental

Sees patterns, light and dark. Focuses eight inches in front of him. Beyond that, vision hazy.

Sensitive to location of sound. Distinguishes volume and pitch, prefers high voice.

Distinguishes length. Quiets when picked up in response to any firm steady pressure.

Distinguishes tastes.

Alert about 3 percent of daylight hours.

Grips object if hand strikes it accidentally. Regards person momentarily.

Stops sucking to look at something.

Shuts out disturbing stimuli.

Social

Personal

Shows excitement, distress.

Is individual in looks, feelings, activity level, and reactions to stimulation.

Interaction

Smiles spontaneously and fleetingly to sensory stimulation, like soft sounds.

Becomes alert to, tries particularly hard to focus on face or voice.

Quiets when picked up.

Searches for nipple.

Cultural

Seven or eight feedings.

Moves bowels often and sporadically.

Sleeps 80 percent of his day in seven or eight daily naps.

THE FIRST MONTH
Family Reorganization

THE FIRST MONTH
Family Reorganization

The first month requires the reordering of baby's day and family life. From the moment of birth, he must learn new ways of getting food and oxygen and of eliminating wastes. His minimal practice with movement and hearing in the womb will amplify enormously in the outside world, while the seeing, tasting, and smelling that he could not practice there will start developing rapidly. In his first week, he must adjust not only to the world outside, he must also reorient himself from the bustling nursery at the hospital to the softer, more personalized atmosphere of home.

And there *you* are. The hospital routine and the joint responsibility that have helped you handle your feelings start vanishing as soon as the nurse helps you dress the baby in your room. She accompanies you to the car and almost ceremoniously resigns the baby to you and your husband, a ritual required by most hospitals. Suddenly, this tiny creature who has just begun to seem real is unmistakably *all yours!* Now you can cuddle him as much as you want, play with him after feedings, and watch him as he sleeps and wakes. With this new control, all your half-swallowed fears, doubts, and unsureness come to the surface.

A new mother who feels this overwhelming joy, responsibility, *and* anxiety is not alone. Every new mother experiences much the same thing. Many feel like weeping and often do—unaccountably. They wonder if they are inadequate or even if their uncontrollable feelings mean they are losing their minds.

You may feel constantly drained. Everything requires more of you than it should and anything out of place provokes you to tears. If you do mobilize yourself to do something constructive, you are exhausted. If you cannot, you are annoyed with yourself. You know your husband would love some notice, but you can barely tolerate any affectionate overture. Yet you feel alone, forsaken, and unwanted. If someone keeps you waiting for more than fifteen minutes, you think it is because you are the most unattractive, uninspiring female in the world. For the first time in your life, you feel like disagreeing with everyone. You call all your friends to see the baby although your doctor has warned you not to because of your fatigue and the risk of infecting the baby. Besides being somewhat depressed and bored, you may actually envy people. Any older woman's calm, experienced handling of the baby is threatening. You contrast her competence with your confusion and helplessness and you wish you could just curl up in a ball in some quiet corner. The baby himself is frightening. He is so demanding with all his crying and seemingly endless eating.

The contrast between your possibly nightmarish fantasies and impatience with the baby and your dreams of being a perfect mother make you want to weep. So does your conviction that other young mothers are doing much better than you. A new mother's physical adjustment and recovery after delivery underlie this kind of behavior and emotion, which some people call post-partum blues. Maybe you will be one of the few lucky ones who more or less skips these blues. Their length will depend on your general physical and emotional health, the amount of support from your family, the difficulties of the birth, and your own drive. For some mothers, the very sight and sounds of home are enough to start their recovery. For others, the big adjustment taxes their physical and emotional reserves and often makes them unable to sleep and eat properly or to control their emotions.

Unfortunately, modern American society does not help much with these blues. Many women feel desperately that they have no one to turn to. The new father knows even less than his wife. Hired help is costly and many mothers feel that a nurse invades the privacy of their homes. Physicians are available only at prescribed times. Even the baby books are no help, glibly asserting that you must always consider your new baby first. Although no one can feel so selfless during a period of such strenuous personal adjustment, the weight of "evidence" may reduce a young woman to feeling like a total loser as a mother.

In fact, the new mother's immediate family is less likely to be helpful than at other times. Her own mother may be suffering with her at long distance and her husband and children may increase their ordinary demands because of their own adjustment to the baby.

The two-year-old you are so eager to see again feels you have deserted him. His interest in the new baby is dutiful and he is terribly afraid you may leave him again. Even his father may seem to have abandoned him for the new intruder. He may be extraordinarily quiet and subdued, aggressive toward you and the baby, or incessantly demanding—showing off and dreaming up annoying mischief to distract you from his rival. His newly mastered toilet habits may disintegrate and he may insist on your feeding him all over again. If you can contain your surprise and shock at his antics, you may understand the reason for them and give him extra cuddling and comfort. Accepting his investigative intrusions with some good humor will probably help him satisfy his curiosity and minimize the chance of repeats. Shoving him away will only increase his feelings of exclusion, hurt and jealousy.

An older child's reactions may be more complex than those of a two- or three-year-old. He may try to handle the family's changed relationships or your preoccupation by hardly noticing *you* at all, imitating you fiercely, and mothering "his" or "her" baby whenever permitted. In a large family, he may wreak his real hostility on a younger child—stimulating him to be naughty and teasing him until he cries with frustration.

Your husband will be making his own adjustments. The minute you arrive home, he begins to rant about everything that went haywire while you were in the hospital. He may resent his mother's or mother-in-law's "invasion" if she is there to help. Secretly he is not at all sure what this new baby is going to do to his relationship with you.

Modern American culture does not help a young father much either. Although hospitals are beginning to allow a man to stay with his wife through labor, only a very few permit him to see his child born. After delivery, wife and child are unavailable to him. He is allowed to see his wife only in prescribed, short doses of time so that she can rest and attend to this stranger—implying that he, her husband, would strain her already limited strength if his selfish wishes were really turned loose. A plate-glass window and hovering nurses keep him from his own baby, whom he can't feel and can hardly see except for his face, which somehow is left unswathed. If he has the nerve to ask to hold his child, he is informed of his status—"alien and unsterile." The first time he really sees the baby is when the nurse undresses him to put on his "going home" clothes.

If you are amused by your husband's amazement with the baby, his inability to accept the scaling skin and jaundice, and his naive fear of touching and holding him, remember you have had several days to become "experienced." He may not have had the chance to voice his fears to anyone. He wonders about acting like a father. Since he has only seen his baby in the nursery, he hardly feels like a parent. As you may be able to tell, he is somewhat nervous. He may feel jealous that he cannot carry the baby as you leave the hospital, or he may be absolutely terrified to. At home, he may want to hold the baby in his arms but does not dare say so, let alone try.

Promote these positive wishes by asking your husband to hold the baby or perhaps help with feeding, bathing, or dressing him. Even if he may not want to do these things himself, your husband will at least know how if the need arises. A young father needs to feel he is doing something. Once he gains self-confidence in handling the baby, his own parenting instinct, different from yours but definitely there, will eventually take over.

During these first weeks at home grandmother can be a real help. Her main assets are her moral support for you and her experience as a mother. In addition, she may assist with baby care, housekeeping, even in alleviating your husband's tension, depending on her relationship with him.

Her role is not easy. Besides her own conflict between needing to be with you and wanting to be at home, she may often face your very natural jealousy. She is a "fair" target for anger, defensiveness, and frustration, while she herself may be struggling to keep her promises to stay in the background and restrain the very human need to give sound advice. She might return home at the end of her stay feeling that she has failed to help you relieve your tension. Yet she can give you and your husband time—time to get yourselves together to mother and father your baby. Nobody can do your job for you. But depending on her tact in presenting her ideas, some of them may get through and help you in her absence.

Creature of Habit?

Meanwhile the baby must adapt just as dramatically. Life in the hospital's newborn nursery is a far cry from a quiet room in a home's nurturing world. He has learned how to defend himself against intense light, the constant noise of busy nurses and screaming infants, and the physical discomfort of impersonal, sometimes rough handling, and of being wet, dirty, and hungry at times that did not fit the schedule of a hospital staff.

For some days after you bring him home, your baby will be a very disorganized little fellow. Most newborns are active at birth, quiet for the next few days, then more active again the first days at home. They cry a lot and eat poorly, frequently, and erratically. If your baby is breast feeding, he may suck for long stretches of thirty to forty minutes at each breast on some days, but only ten to twenty minutes on others. He probably won't quiet with handling as well as he will later. He wakes fitfully, breathes irregularly, sneezes, chokes, spits up, vomits occasionally, and startles frequently.

According to Dr. Peter H. Wolff, a neurophysiologist at the Massachusetts Institute of Technology, a month-old baby sleeps more than he does anything else, cries more than he is active, and divides the small time he is awake between drowsiness and alertness. He sleeps much more than you do, at least twelve and usually about fourteen hours. While his eyes may be shut for more than that, he will actually be awake and can receive and respond to stimulation.

He also sleeps differently from you. You have only two sleep phases; the baby has three, though his sleep phases do not differ as sharply as yours. His sleep may be light or restless, periodic, or deep. His deep sleep features no activity, a reposed face, regular breathing, firmly closed eyelids, and little response to stimulation.

Neonates are mostly light sleepers. Scientists know this because they have recorded the distinctive brain wave pattern and greater body movement associated with dreaming. At birth about half your baby's sleep is restless and 20 to 30 percent is deep. His level of sleep fluctuates according to an internal clock. He may rouse in regular three-hour cycles, or cry out more sporadically, raise his head, move to the top of the crib, and quiet. Almost all of his deep sleep episodes are about twenty minutes long. By about the second week, this timing is so regular that you can predict when your baby will wake or become restless. Gradually this whole pattern reverses itself so that the eight-month-old approximates the adult's sleep pattern of 50 to 70 percent deep sleep and 20 to 25 percent dream time.

When your baby is sleeping lightly, he is more susceptible to inner and outer stimulation, and you can see all kinds of behavior. He whimpers, grimaces, smiles, sneers, frowns, pouts, mouths rhythmically, breathes irregularly, and if you watch very closely, you can see his eyes darting beneath the lids. Sleep smiles are different from the social ones you will see a bit later when your baby's eyes are bright and his whole face lights up to a voice or face. A sleep smile, which is often stimulated by sounds, just works the muscles of his lower face.

Newborns also catnap, rather than sleep in long stretches. The longest newborn sleep period is about four to five hours. Usually seven or eight naps alternate with wakeful states ranging from a drowsiness that looks like drugged stupor to wild flailing of arms and legs and frantic crying.

A baby can actively squirm, kick, or suck on his fist as much as twelve hours a day. A few causes of his increased activity are fairly apparent. A baby grows more active before feeding and urination. He also becomes very overwhelmed by pain or other disturbing outside stimulation and sometimes sets up a cycle of activity that only you can interrupt. His activity upsets him and further sensitizes him to the offensive stimulation. The more sensitive he becomes, the more vigorously he struggles. Some bursts of activity seem triggered by fatigue, long periods of lying awake, or looking around.

Some psychological causes also seem at work. Loosely wrapped swaddling can rouse a baby to outrage even though it is not painful, while he calms down when well swaddled.

While all this activity may look pointless to you, it is very important to your baby's growth. These basic movements will later differentiate and become coordinated with the baby's reflexes to become part of his developing motor patterns.

Why Do Babies Cry?

Crying and fretting often go with your baby's thrashing about—a combination he is most likely to break into if he is hungry, thirsty, tired, or frustrated. Crying is really his first social communication. It is not terribly sophisticated but it is useful. Partly because it is a distress signal of children and adults, partly because it is irritating, partly because of instinct, mother usually comes running to discover what is making her baby cry.

On some days your baby may cry for twenty to thirty minutes four or five times a day before feedings, sleeping, or elimination. You can modify this before naps by placing your baby on his tummy. This position helps him control the startling that still accompanies his crying. On other days the baby's crying, squirming, and fussing before sleeping in the evening can last from one to three hours at a time. The longer periods may follow a noisy, busy day, a weekend when father is at home, or a "blue period" for mother.

After lying for hours looking around quietly, he may slowly begin whimpering. At first he can be talked to and will become alert and stare at your face for several minutes. You can rock him for almost thirty minutes before he tires and begins to wail again. But sooner or later he will reach a point when no comforting really succeeds more than briefly. Play, rocking, swaddling, changing his diapers, feeding him to be sure he isn't hungry are all useless. He will continue to cry for long stretches, tapering off to deep, shuddering sobs before sleep. These periods may be his attempts to discharge enough energy so that he can settle down. Infants who fuss are more likely to sleep for long periods at night.

This timing at day's end is not entirely haphazard. Dr. Anna Freud writes of the falling to pieces of a baby's ego at the end of a day. The family's fatigue, the mother's own ego disintegration, and the expectant excitement around a father's homecoming all contribute.

Studies on infant crying show that environmental tension does add to the length and intensity of crying spells. A baby can tune in his family's feelings. When his mother is tired or tense, he is impossibly fussy. When she is rested and un- harried, he is delightfully responsive. Studies show that crying for "unknown causes" decreases sharply when a baby gets more mothering—handling, talking to, looking, and listening.

Do not feel badly if you cannot soothe your baby as quickly or easily as you expect. There may be nothing wrong with either you or him. Some crying may simply be inevitable and necessary. Psychologists tell us a "bad" day of crying and fussing may indicate tension before a thrust into a new developmental stage. The good, quiet, peaceful days are usually those when your baby is operating on the same level and not responding to any kind of change.

Then, too, babies differ as much in what quiets them as in how much stimulation excites them. You might try another method of soothing him—some babies like crooning, some prefer being rocked, some like being held at the shoulder, others enjoy being cuddled, still others like sucking.

Babies tend to form attachments on the basis of the kind of stimulation they want and get. A baby may prefer the uncle who rocks him to the one who tickles, just as he may prefer one voice to another. You might work out a system of letting him cry for twenty minutes, then picking him up and cuddling him, getting bubbles up by feeding him sugar water, and putting him back to bed to cry again. Handling him calmly with this routine may quiet him.

Some doctors find that babies held in close contact over their mother's hearts cry less. The heartbeat seems to soothe them, possibly because in the womb they have already heard their mother's heart. Dr. Lee Salk of the New York Hospital—Cornell Medical Center has some fascinating things to say about this. Babies respond to music as early as the first month, probably because the tempo of music, from the most primitive to the most modern, is usually between fifty and one hundred and fifty beats per minute, essentially the range of the human heartbeat. Most mothers, both right and left-handed, do in fact hold their babies on their left side, including mothers in sculpture and paintings from Italian Renaissance to Henry Moore and Picasso.

The one-month-old is alert only a small portion of the time he is awake. Dr. Wolff clocked about three hours of intermittent alertness from about thirty hours of wakefulness a week. This is your baby's natural playtime, the best time for a little sociability, a little getting to know each other. The baby can lie quietly on his back, alert and listening, for as much as an hour or as little as a couple of minutes half a dozen times a day. He will quiet more readily and is more responsive to novel sights, sounds, and stimulation after a changing, feeding, and bubbling than before, when hunger and other physical discomforts interfere.

Since the first increases in the length of your baby's alertness occur only when he is comfortable, relieving these irritations is most important. Short as they are, your baby's alert periods are prerequisites for more advanced learning. As Dr. Howard A. Moss of the National Institute of Mental

Health says, "The amount of time an infant spends at a given level of consciousness is clearly going to influence the way he experiences the world, the types of discriminations he makes, and his level of mental organization." For example, the important ability to follow and observe something carefully develops primarily when your baby is alert.

Some investigators have even speculated that visual stimulation in the first four months facilitates the growth of the visual apparatus. A stimulating environment allows the month-old baby to organize his responses to external events rather than just his physical needs. His attention to an interesting taste, smell, sight, or sound actually controls diffuse, aimless activity. When the eyelids of a drowsy baby finally close, spontaneous energy discharges occur which seem inhibited as long as his eyes are open.

Since the baby's alertness is apt to evaporate as soon as an interesting spectacle is removed, you can keep him alert by focusing his attention on an interesting sight, such as a moving toy or a mobile, or a sound, perhaps a bell toy. In fact, for a tiny baby just as for us, meaningful encounters with the environment are one critical way to maintain alertness. Dr. Wolff found that a provocative, interesting environment may alert even a fussy or drowsy baby. Even if it does not, as long as his lids remain open, a drowsy baby appears to register his sight experiences, which seem to impress him. There may be a whole range of seemingly meaningless stimuli that, despite the baby's apparent indifference, contribute to his learning and behavior. After all, you can read a book or watch a movie without indicating to anyone what you have learned and without changing your visible behavior in any way.

Babies seem to *choose* to stay awake for stimulation and activity. Once they have been fed and their physical comfort attended to, they certainly do not need to stay awake. All *you* need to know is how much sleep, stimulation, and activity your baby seems to need. Babies are individualists in these matters as in everything else. You will soon find what amount of excitation your baby can cope with, as well as the method of soothing that your baby responds to best.

If you are in touch with your baby, you will respond to his preferences. When he is tense and highly aroused, you may soothe him. When he is quiet and alert, you can play with, talk to, and show him things because it pleases both you and the baby. The important point is that if a baby's tensions are relieved as they arise, he soon gets the idea that the world is a good place, and the people in it worth getting to know.

Breast Feeding or the Bottle?

Babies also spend a lot of time eating. It is a very important part of their day. The specific feeding practice—breast or bottle, schedule or demand—matters less emotionally than the context of the mother-child relationship. The only kind of feeding generally frowned on is propping the bottle because the baby misses the warm security and pleasure of human contact. Some pediatricians feel this lack can seriously interfere with his chance for normal psychological development. Being alone with a bottle is a cold way for an infant to experience such an important daily event and forces him to rely on his own resources at feeding time. This reliance is apt to prolong and intensify his attachment to his bottle since he has had to turn to it as his primary gratification when feeding.

With that exception, the most thorough scientific attempt to date to compare the effects of breast feeding with those of bottle feeding concluded that factors like the sex of the baby and the warmth or rejection of the mother were more important than the style of feeding. What seems critical is the kind and amount of sensory and social stimulation a mother gives her baby and her gratification of his needs. Bottle feeding and breast feeding both give the baby the security and tactile stimulation of being held and supported, as well as the social stimulation of being talked to and played with.

Even so, there are decided differences between breast and bottle feeding. Breast feeding gives the most opportunity for close contact between mother and child. The greatest asset to the mother may be a kind of peace within herself during and after nursing. Mothers say they feel they have given their babies a real part of themselves, have communicated on the baby's terms for a short time, and do not feel guilty leaving them for the next few hours to tend to other children and responsibilities.

Breast feeding also gives the baby certain physiological advantages. It prevents feeding problems, allergic reactions, and constipation, and gives him antibodies that partially protect him against infection.

If you are breast feeding, be aware that the tension and fatigue surrounding homecoming may reduce the amount of milk you had in the hospital. A mother who wants to nurse must rest and relax. You should let grandmother, husband, or sitter help, and not worry or try to do everything yourself a large part of your first week home. It may make the difference between success and failure in feeding.

Offer your baby an occasional bottle in the first few months to familiarize him with it. Otherwise he may refuse a complementary formula when you are ill or lack milk for one reason or another. In spite of initial refusals, most babies will take a formula in an emergency.

A nursing mother should also understand that half-conscious envy prompts the undermining digs she will hear from other women. Dr. Brazelton indicates that comments like "Are you *still* nursing?" "The baby's too fat (or too thin)," "Haven't you started solids yet?"—all reflect competitive feelings. Even a contemporary or a grandmother who has nursed her own children and enjoyed it may envy this delightful unity.

But you need not feel guilty about deciding not to nurse your baby. You may have your own well-founded reasons. A physician's attempts to dislodge such feelings with whatever good intent can be a mistake. You may feel you can leave your baby more readily with your husband or sitter if he is conditioned to the bottle, which is true. You may also feel that breast feeding will interfere with your time with your other children. On the other hand, you could reason that since breast feeding does so much for the new baby in such a short time, you can spend time with your older child without fear of shortchanging the baby. Some mothers worry about their older children being more disturbed by breast feeding. Actually what disturbs an older child is any kind of close attention to the new baby. Ultimately, whether you breast feed or not is in no way as important to your baby as a good start with his mother.

Scheduling or Self-demand?

Like breast versus bottle, scheduling versus self-demand is another nutritional issue among infancy specialists. Scheduling may simply be impossible if your baby wakes irregularly and requires differing amounts of food. If these are not problems, too-rigid scheduling may be. It may mean the baby sometimes eats before he wants to, in which case he either takes very little or is almost impossible to feed, then wakes early for the next feeding. It may also mean he eats after his hunger pains have become so severe that his tension level peaks. Since hunger is one of your baby's most critical drives, it will interfere with important things like sleep and learning. Hunger initially augments but then disorganizes a baby's goal-directed activities, such as bringing his hand to his mouth. Hunger causes a shift from deep to restless sleep, to waking, to violent crying and wild activity. A meal under such conditions is likely to be anything but pleasurable.

When a mother feeds her baby entirely on demand, she lets him pick his own part of the twenty-four-hour cycle in which to eat and extend his sleep. It can be troublesome at first. You may have many responsibilities, including the needs of your husband and other children, household tasks or outside work, which actually prevent you from always feeding your baby strictly on demand.

But self-demand eventually becomes self-scheduling. The

baby has a built-in tendency to stabilize both his eating and sleeping patterns. As they mature, few babies are unwilling to adjust to a long sleep at night when the rest of the family needs it. Your baby will also eat larger amounts less frequently. The best solution is probably a compromise, a modified demand-feeding schedule where you keep track of the intervals at which the baby seems to get hungry and plan to feed him around those times.

Babies usually develop fairly regular hunger patterns of their own. Some babies are better suited to a four-hour feeding schedule, others to being fed every three hours, still others to two and one-half or three hours in the daytime, but four or five hours at night. By waking your baby during the day for his feedings, you can gently pressure him to sleep during the evenings when you don't awaken him. Your consistency is important because abrupt changes can lead to disorganization and distress. Once a baby gets used to a particular schedule you can expect more activity and crying in the last hour before feeding. Restless motion, mouthing his fist, or finally screaming and searching for the nipple are your cues that he's learned to expect food at a certain time. By the middle of the first year, he will adapt quite naturally to a three-meal-a-day routine, just as he has become accustomed to sleeping through the night and napping only twice a day.

Do not be anxious or impatient if your baby is a slow eater or eats less than you think he should. Conviction about the value of demand-feeding is pointless if you become so irritable that you inadvertently handle your baby poorly and make his meals unpleasant for you both. Babies differ widely at birth in the rate and vigor of their sucking and in the amount of food they require. Your baby's feeding needs, like his other needs, are not the same as those of any other baby. Choose the way that makes a pleasant situation for you and him—one in which you will enjoy each other's company. If he is not hungry, put the bottle aside or remove the breast, play with him, and talk to him. Whether or not he has that last ounce is less consequential than his feelings about the experiences the world and its people offer him.

Progress Report

The drama of a new baby's homecoming and the upheaval

of all the principals around him are by no means exaggerated. The first three weeks of life away from the hospital are probably the longest and most depleting of a family's relationship with its newest member. Most families suffer disruption as everyone regroups toward the goal of being a bigger-by-one family. But gradually you will regain your physical and emotional strength. Your first-week slump may even be a necessary part of adapting to motherhood. Even the baby, although he still seems to spend a lot of time sleeping, has been busy every moment adjusting to life on the outside. He has had lots of new jobs to do simultaneously and you will probably have noted many changes.

He is heavier than he was when he was born, although he only regained his birth weight somewhere around the tenth day of life.

He is still a little bundle of reflexes, but he's not so limp anymore. This is partly because the brain itself is firmer and less gelatinous. His muscles are firmer. Millions and millions of new connections have grown between millions and millions of nerve cells in his organs, as well as his muscles.

His eyes do not seem to roll around in his head so much; the twelve tiny muscles controlling them are better organized, and he is learning to control them and to focus his eyes a little more quickly and often. He tries so hard to focus, particularly to a face or toward a voice, that his eyes sometimes cross, his body shivers, and he begins to hiccough with the effort. He is beginning to "reach" with his eyes.

He breathes more regularly, and chokes, vomits, trembles, and startles less. In a few weeks, his spontaneous startles during sleep will have been reduced to occasional twitches in his face, hands, and feet.

Instead of total unpredictableness, he may now move his bowels only once, but probably no more than four times a day on waking from sleep.

Feeding and Sleeping Patterns

Waking and sleeping states differ more clearly with fewer gradations between. A primitive pattern sets in. The baby wakes most when he is hungry, then cries, feeds, becomes alert, grows drowsy, and sleeps again.

Other patterns are beginning to stabilize more and more. By the third to fifth week, your baby may reduce his seven or eight feedings to five or six over a twenty-four-hour day, with four-hour stretches between feedings during the day.

From seven or eight periods of sleep in every twenty-four hours, he has probably reduced the daily naps to three or four and combined two of them into one five or six-hour night-time sleep, possibly after the 10 P.M. feeding. He is establishing a simple cycle of quiet and unquiet, night and day. By two weeks he takes as much as eighteen ounces of milk daily, increasing to twenty-four or twenty-five ounces by four weeks.

In contrast to the excessive crying and accompanying uncoordinated movements of the first ten days or so of life, his total crying time may begin to decrease as you handle him with more understanding and less anxiety. His interested, alert periods will lengthen. He has learned to mouth his fist or suck his thumb and can shorten the crying and fussing himself. As time goes on, he may differentiate the first two fingers of one hand and learn to suck on them with loud smacks of comfort. After his explosive bouts, he seems to eat and sleep better.

By now you are quite good at understanding his different cries of hunger, discomfort, pain, or boredom. You will also recognize some new sounds—throaty noises called cooing.

Another emotion is emerging—enjoyment. He cries when wet and quiets when changed. He enjoys his bath, probably because of the handling involved.

A new kind of crying just before he falls asleep signals a new stage of development, a readiness for experiences. He wants to be held, carried, or propped so he can look around.

You may also notice that his fixed staring at things—sometimes as long as ten to fifteen minutes—is followed by a new kind of behavior. He becomes excited when he sees a person or toy. He moves his arms and legs, pants, vocalizes, and even smiles, with a kind of readiness to respond.

A baby does not yet distinguish between his actions and their results. The world is hungry, or warm, or wet, or feels good. Things just seem to appear and disappear before the new infant, as though he were seeing them, says Dr. Jean Piaget, through the window of a moving train. But by four weeks, he will begin to repeat actions for their own sake; for instance, kicking for the pleasure of it.

Although there is still no "I" and "me," he is beginning

to distinguish a few people around him by their voices. His face brightens when his brother or sister talk softly to him. He recognizes his mother's voice particularly, though he often seems less content with it. He may stop what he's doing, slowly turn toward her voice, mouth his fist, and frown, squirm, or fuss. His father may more readily produce a smile, as well as the most prolonged period of responsiveness. This difference may be based on an early association of cues, or a kind of discrimination. Father may well be more relaxed, the exchange with his baby more pure than mother's, who is distracted by other children and her caretaking. Father means play, but mother means business (feeding). By this time, all the cues of feeding, her voice, smells, and presence have heightened significance.

Adding it all up, the baby is getting ready for the surge of growth and development ahead.

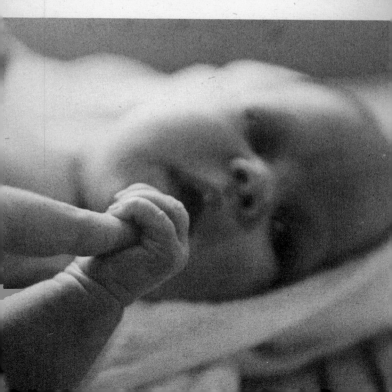

Motor

Large

Virtually all arm, leg, and hand movements are still reflexive. On back, tonic neck reflex (fencer's position) still predominates. Thrusts arms and legs in play.

Unsupported head sags, flops forward or backward.
On tummy, turns head to clear nose from bed; lifts head briefly.

Rolls part way to side from back.

Sitting

May hold head in line with back when pulled to sitting position.

Small

Generally keeps hands fisted or slightly open. When fingers are pried open, grasps handle of spoon or rattle, but drops it quickly.

Stares at object, does not reach.

Coordinates eyes more.

Language

Active

Besides crying, begins small throaty sounds.

Passive

Responds to voice.

Please do not regard this chart as a rigid timetable. Babies are unpredictable. Some perform an activity earlier or later than the chart indicates.

Growth Chart

Mental

Prefers patterns to any kind of color, brightness, or size.

Alert about one out of every ten hours. Vague, indirect regard and expression most of waking hours.

Coordinates eyes sideways and up and down in regarding light or object. Follows toy from side to center of his body. Becomes excited when he sees a person or toy. Regards them only if in his line of vision. "Loses" them if at center of eye too long.

Remembers object that reappears within two and one-half seconds. Expects feedings at certain intervals.

Quiets to being held or seeing faces. Cries deliberately for assistance.

Reflexes become more efficient.

Social

Personal

Responds positively to comfort and satisfaction; negatively to pain.

Interaction

May smile back at face or voice.

Eyes fix on mother's face in response to her smile.
Makes eye to eye contact.
Regards faces and quiets down.

Adjusts posture to body of person holding him. Grasp, clasps people. Roots and sucks at breast.

May recognize parent's voice.

Most of the time expression is vague and impassive.

Cultural

Daily patterns of sleeping, crying, and eating are highly disorganized. Two night feedings. Five or six daily.

Moves bowels three or four times daily.

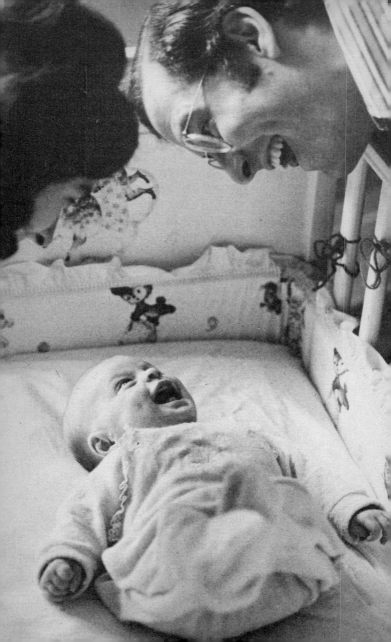

THE
SECOND
MONTH
The Smiler

THE SECOND MONTH
The Smiler

After your baby's busy adjustment to life in a new world during his first month, the relative calm of the second gives him a chance to grow dramatically and to socialize more. Not just a new plaything, he is becoming entrenched as a family member. He is also growing before your very eyes. In these next few months, some babies gain as much as two pounds a month. Your one-month-old is beginning to learn to control his head. It is steadier now and he holds it up occasionally at a 45-degree angle to look around for a few minutes. Voluntary grasping is already replacing his reflex grasp.

When he is calm, his movements are rarely jerky or staccato. But when he is upset or hungry, he reverts immediately to his earlier jumps and jerks. His chin quivers and his arms and legs tremble. A screaming child or a door slamming down the hall will make him startle, throw out his arms and legs, and arch his back. Even so, his movements become smoother every day and simple patterns of personal style and development surface. A quiet baby will continue his steady course of development, sleep a lot, remain quiet when awake, and probably eat well. An active baby may make you feel you are on a mad roller-coaster as he careens through his developmental ups and downs. Most exciting, your baby is beginning to learn to adapt some of his inborn reflex abilities to new situations and to look at people and smile.

Routines and Regularity

By this time, your two-month-old may be quite regular in his demands. He may drink as much as thirty-five ounces of milk a day. He wants his daytime feedings (still as long as forty minutes each) at four-hour intervals and he is not one to let you forget them. His crying can become so insistent, it resounds throughout the house and disturbs everyone.

The baby probably will be sleeping through the night feeding by now so that by the fifth week his night-time sleep lasts as long as seven hours. This brings his regular daily feedings to five, with perhaps an occasional bottle once in a while at night or during the day. At seven weeks, he will sleep seven and one-half to eight hours until six or later in the morning. Usually babies will sleep through the night feeding when they are around eleven pounds in weight. Some gain this weight earlier and some later. Some two-month-olds, especially quiet ones, will still demand a feeding every four hours day or night because they do not tire enough to lengthen their night's sleep. For some, almost nothing will change this pattern except the baby himself.

During the day your baby will probably be wide awake for as many as ten hours now—taking one- to three-hour naps. An active baby's wiry movements may fill all ten of them. When put on his back, he fairly whirrs with activity, cycling his arms around his head, bicycling his legs, and twisting his body from side to side. He has a little trouble with more refined movements. If his cycling arms have to zero in on his mouth, he has to stab repeatedly to get his thumb into it.

Sometimes precocious physical activity can get the baby into trouble simply because you do not expect such prowess. His arching and flexing can turn him completely over onto his tummy or pull him off a table or bed. The mother of an active infant should start to check possible hazards as early as the second month. She also has to consider how to keep him covered at night. Since movement is an important outlet for an active baby, a sleeping bag is probably the best solution because his arms are free and he can move unhampered. If he has to spend at least half his twenty-four hours in sleep, he should not be harnessed or tied down. His freedom is important to his happiness, his physical development, and maybe even his eventual view of the world.

Just as he begins to eat and sleep regularly, your baby will still cry at fairly predictable intervals every day. At the end of the day, he is likely to fuss on and off for about an hour. Some babies almost totally disintegrate at day's end. They may stiffen, cut down their activity, and seem to concentrate their energy in deep breaths ending in bursts of steady, high-pitched wails. Their color may change to purple and they may even seem to stop breathing, then quiet, yawn, and start crying again. (Infants before the second year will not actually stop breathing long enough to pass out.)

Nothing works to quiet this kind of baby. He will probably refuse to fit into any position offered and try wriggling out of your arms. Vigorous rocking or rapid walking with him in your arms may quiet him briefly, but as soon as these efforts stop, he will cry strenuously again. Research conducted under the direction of Dr. Lewis P. Lipsitt of Brown University by one of his associates, Dr. Leonore DeLucia, found that rocking a child when he cried only reinforced and encouraged greater periods of crying; whereas rocking him when he was quiet encouraged more quiet periods and less fussing.

Hunger is not the problem. You might be able to make him take an ounce or two of formula as he fusses, but he really is uninterested and usually spits it up as he becomes more and more active. He is more likely to eat at the end of his crying jag.

There is no magic way to interfere with this period. Babies this age cry a lot because they sense the frustrating imbalance between their sophisticated sensory apparatus and their almost total physical disability. Time and maturation will take care of this. Several days may pass without much fretting, followed by a third or fourth of nonstop sound as if the baby were making up for lost time.

Actually the baby is beginning to compensate for his crying jags and that first month of fussing and disorganization. His smile, a thoroughly ingratiating response, has appeared, and other positive emotions counter-balance his expressions of discomfort or disgust. By two months, the expression of disgust is a full-fledged grimace to new bitter, sour, or salty tastes. Some infants even gag, choke, turn purple, frown, clench their jaws, and turn away. Now, however, the baby also responds to attention and seems to feel it is desirable enough to try to get. Most babies' responsive periods after feedings have lengthened, for some to as much as an hour and a half. After he has taken the first part of his feeding, he may pause to look around or to smile into your face. Although exasperating for a hurried mother, this play is wonderful to a baby. As Dr. Jacob L. Gewirtz of the National Institute of Health says, "The biologically satisfied infant is quite the opposite of the passive and unresponsive being he is pictured to be in the widely held theories of Freud. The highly responsive infant actively, regularly and extensively interacts with his environment when his organic needs are satisfied. In fact he seems to seek stimulation which is ever more complex as he moves to each higher stage of development."

When people are around, the baby can gradually work up a slow smile and a bicycling performance. He performs his acrobatics most adroitly for an audience. When people are particularly sensitive to him, he can keep responding for as long as twenty minutes before he disintegrates with exhaustion. An active baby will arch, turn, twist, and kick so much that even you feel exhausted. Even when he is fussy, a brother or sister can amuse him. Alone, he has his own ways to quiet himself—sucking his fist or fingers, turning his head, looking at a fluttering curtain, or listening to the sounds of mother. Almost inperceptibly, his fussing slips into sociability, and usually by the end of the second month your baby is directing a lot of his energy elsewhere. For most parents, the beginning of this change is apparent only in retrospect. You may still tense expectantly for the evening fusses long after baby has turned them off himself.

Some babies begin showing preferences for one side of the body rather than the other or for a sleep position. The baby may suck his right first, look out of the crib's right side, and keep his head to the right in his infant chair. By the sixth week, the constant pressure may begin to flatten his skull. When your pediatrician determines that muscular or neurological problems, such as a shortened muscle or damaged nerves in the neck, are not the reasons for this preference, you might try the following. Turn the baby's crib so he has to look out to the left to see into the room and look at people, or hang toys in the crib slightly to the left so he must turn his head to look at them. Raising the mattress an inch or two on the right side so that gravity helps the baby turn his head to the left may also help. You need not worry about permanent head flattening because a baby's head rounds as it grows during his first year and a half. Pressure on the flat side will be alleviated as soon as he sits up.

If he is nursing, your baby may also prefer one breast, and fuss, cry, or turn away when put to the other. This favoritism may relate to an inborn preference for keeping his head to one or the other side or even to a position in the womb to which he became accustomed. If putting the baby on the unfavored side first does not correct his preference, try to nurse him lying down or hold him in a more vertical position.

Most infants strongly prefer a particular sleeping position, such as lying on the tummy. Some infants seek a corner or the top of their crib to press their head against before they settle down. Analysts have labeled this an attempt to return to the womb with the head engaged in the pelvis. If your

baby does not fuss much or tell you in other ways, this preference may become apparent only when he will not nap
unless he is turned on his favorite side.

Mothers often try to change this urge for a sleep position
because they have heard that one position is unsafe or
another may hurt his legs or feet. Actually, satisfying the
infant's natural preference for a comfortable sleep pattern is
far better than tussling with the pros and cons of others
advocated in the baby literature. Infants, unless they are
sick, will not choke on their backs. On their stomachs, they
will not bury themselves in their bedclothes unless too many
bedclothes are in the crib. (Heavy pajamas and sleeping bags
in the winter preclude the need for many bedclothes.) Some
pediatricians feel that orthopedic doctors overrate sleep positions as the cause of foot problems.

Early Learning

Your baby is beginning to associate and discriminate between many types of behavior. Placing him on his tummy may
initiate screams of rage because it is the position he is put
in for sleep, which he dislikes. If you put him on his back, he
quiets immediately.

He associates certain people with particular behavior. He
seems to have learned that if he screams a particular scream
you appear. Before his meal, he sucks his fingers but as
soon as he is in your arms, his hands are of no interest and
his sucking efforts are directed to the nipple. If you are
breast feeding him, he may refuse to take a bottle from you
because he associates you with a different kind of feeding.
It is not that he inherently dislikes cow's milk because his
father can and does feed him from a bottle. But the association is so strong that his father can feed him only if you are
out of the room and quiet. Even the sound of your voice in
another room may make the baby refuse the bottle.

The baby concentrates his full powers to see, to pay attention to all kinds of cues, and to turn his head just to keep
them in sight. Possibly size of the object makes a difference.
In 1964, B. G. Bower, a scientist, indicated that two-month-
olds do in fact distinguish object size.

Drs. Richard Held and Burton White of Harvard University
also indicate that flexibility of visual response begins at
about the middle of the second month. The eye's lens begins

to adjust itself to the distance of an object. By four months of age, the lens of the eye comfortably accommodates objects at different distances.

Experimental data indicate that two-month-olds distinguish between sights and sounds. A newborn will not bother to move his head up and down to follow a sound, but he will try to do so for a gaudy bauble or a moving light. Two-month-olds also prefer people to objects and respond differently to them. Babies as they mature change their preferences from straight patterns, such as stripes, to curved configurations more like those of the human face. They grow still before turning their heads to a ball or a chime, while their response to people seems more immediate.

Your baby can recognize your voice now—even in a noisy, crowded room—but frowns and averts his head and eyes when a stranger talks to him. Although a sitter can try everything to quiet him, he may become fussy and inconsolable while you are gone. Though he probably cannot tell the difference between your face and hers yet, he can differentiate her handling of him from yours.

Even more exciting, he is beginning to acquire the idea of place. To see if three- to eight-week-old babies understood that a person's voice comes from where the person is, researchers at Radcliff College used two stereo speakers that separated the sounds of a voice from its source. The babies were seated before a glass partition separating them from their mothers just two feet away. As long as the speakers were balanced so that the mother's voice seemed to come directly from her, the infants remained content. But when the phase relationship between the speakers made the voice appear to come from a different spot, the babies cried, looked around, became agitated, and clearly indicated by their frustration that their expectations were being countered.

A baby also senses differences in his parents' proximity to him even when he is only half awake. For this reason most pediatricians and psychologists agree that the baby should not sleep in the same room as his parents. When he does, he cries out for them, requires more attention, and sleeps poorly.

Through visual and more active exploration, your baby becomes familiar with his surroundings and with particular objects, essential learning for all organisms. His perusal of the world in which he lives gives the context for all subsequent learned or instinctive behavior. Even if the baby can retain his newly acquired information only a short time, what he learns during sequences of quickly forgotten visual experiences may have a cumulative effect that lasts through hours of visual exploration. The accumulated knowledge then allows the baby to concentrate his attention on less familiar, unexplored parts of his world and so speeds the acquisition of information.

Even sucking, a reflex ability infants are born with, becomes a learning exercise for your baby. By two months, he sucks for food, pleasure, and learning. At this stage, fifteen to twenty minutes on each breast or twenty minutes on a bottle gives a baby as much sucking as he needs for nutrition. He can get at least half of that during the first five minutes, when his sucking is most vigorous. As early as three weeks, an infant begins sucking his own fingers for more than food. It is not because he does not have enough mothering. A baby with the best possible relationship with his mother returns to finger sucking even after the most pleasant feedings because of the enjoyment it gives him. In fact, the happiest babies often suck the most. Some scientists have speculated that the baby is actually attempting to recreate the sensuous experience for himself and to compensate for the loss of his mother. As Dr. Brazelton points out, "When finger sucking is invested with the memory of satisfying feeding, the contact with mother, and gratification of the need for sucking, it becomes very important to your baby."

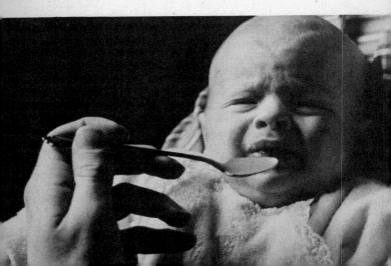

Sucking quiets infants. It reduces hunger pangs and relieves muscle tension. Experiments have shown that the more active a baby is generally, the more vigorous his sucking, and the more it calms him. Although he may occasionally lose his comfort source in a startle response, the baby will try to get his hand back to his mouth so he can suck again. Sucking on thumbs or fingers rather than pacifiers has the advantage of satisfying the need for sucking independently of mother or the object itself. Pacifiers are not inherently "bad" replacements. However, the way in which mothers use them can be harmful. Some mothers overuse pacifiers to "keep the baby occupied" or to alleviate their half-conscious anxiety about the baby's self-sufficiency. Babies of such mothers can grow fat and passive by two years of age, happy only when their mouths are full. In these cases the use of pacifiers may reflect the mother's need for a "crutch." Although some mothers do feel a bit jealous of this first sign of "self-sufficiency," the very fact that your baby has learned a way to satisfy himself is a source of pride.

The mouth is also used for exploration. Sucking is not only pleasurable, it is one of the first "learning" experiences. For the first weeks of life, your baby's mouth is one of his main channels of perception. In fact it is the universal all-purpose sense organ, although babies differ in their styles of using it. Some spit, others drool, some suck vigorously, others more passively.

Right from the start, infant sucking moves toward being fitted into many enterprises. The relationship between sucking and looking, for example, goes through three phases. At birth and for some days after, the infant sucks with eyes shut tight because he cannot handle more than one activity at a time. If the infant looks, tracks an object visually, or listens, he stops sucking. In fact, this disruption has been used as a measure of his attention. On the other hand, sucking reduces eye movements and so limits the baby's information intake. As sucking quiets him, he can focus more energy on one activity, like looking around a room and absorbing what he sees, and less on the random movements of his body. Unless an active baby can slow the rather frantic activity that absorbs his energies, he might not have time to add to his important visual development. The more practice a baby gets in doing one thing at a time, the better he may organize the neural patterns involved in a particular activity, and the better he can move to the next behavior he has to learn.

By nine weeks, or thirteen at the latest, the infant begins to suck in bursts and looks during pauses. He may remain generally "aimed" toward the source of stimulation while sucking, but his eyes are not fixed or "locked" onto the object. Finally, often as early as two months and usually before four, the baby seems able to look and suck at once. Sucking's lessening preemption of other activities may belong to a general decrease in one-track behavior and a move toward the exciting and uniquely human ability to concentrate on more than one thing at a time. As Dr. Jerome S. Bruner comments, "Sucking not only serves inborn functions like nutrition, pain reduction, and exploration, it can also be diverted to intelligent instrumental activity that evolution could not possibly have preordained."

Mrs. Ilze Kalnins, a graduate student at Harvard's Center for Cognitive Studies, has shown that five- and six-week-old infants plainly work for visual clarity. While watching a lively color film of an Eskimo mother playing games with her baby in a snug igloo, infants changed their rate of sucking on a pacifier to bring the picture into focus on a lighted screen. The typical six-week-old learns first to "suck the picture into focus," but the moment it is in focus, his interested looking inhibits sucking, thus blurring the picture. The infant resolves his conflict between two good things by sucking without looking until the picture is in focus, then looking and sucking for a brief period. When he stops sucking and the picture blurs, he averts his gaze immediately. Gradually, the infant increases the time during which he can do two things at once—suck and look—and reduces the pauses between sucks to only four seconds. When conditions were reversed so that sucking blurred the picture, the babies learned to stop sucking on the pacifier and to lengthen the pauses between sucks to about eight seconds. Finally, the infant shifts from his usual sucking to a kind of mouthing which keeps the nipple less active. This reduced form of sucking allows him to satisfy his curiosity and to return to full sucking more efficiently than a full stop would. This "place-holding," as Dr. Bruner calls it, is a sequentially organized, adaptive strategy. It is the first signal of a mental skill that shows itself later in manual dexterity and language learning. Watch for it when your baby holds a toy with one hand and explores it with the other.

"Smiley"

For most parents, the most exciting second-month event is their baby's smile. If you look at or talk to a baby this age, he is very likely to activate his limbs and trunk and gurgle and coo until his whole body "smiles."

At this point, he is not really smiling at *you*. He is smiling at a human face. All over the world, real social smiling begins between two and eight weeks of life. Babies may even smile at human contact earlier. Some old-schoolers insist that first-month smiling is only a response to stomach upset. Some doctors say it signals tension discharge as the baby relaxes and falls asleep. But many have noted spontaneous smiles to human sounds or touches in the first twenty-four hours of life. One psychologist, Dr. Peter Wolff of M.I.T., suggests that smiles begin as barometers of mild surprise. Newborns smile to soft sounds during light sleep, but startle during deep sleep. A drowsy one-month-old will either smile or startle when a moving object suddenly appears before him. Perhaps mother's face appearing above her baby first draws a smile because of its surprise value.

Babies just naturally and instinctively smile at faces—pictured, sculpted, or real. Experiments show that infants under two months of age look longest at linear patterns rather than at curved patterns reminiscent of the human face. Presented with pictures of the human face, newborns do not prefer any particular arrangement of features. But from two to three months of age, babies prefer correct arrangement most consistently. (Remember that they can see much better, too.) They also suddenly develop a strong preference for three-dimensional heads rather than pictures or photographs of faces.

Babies smile most between two and five months because their smiling is still fairly independent of their social environment. Dr. Jacob L. Gewirtz of the National Institute of Mental Health established that two-month-olds stare at, grow active, vocalize, and quickly smile to unresponsive human faces. As early as 1946, Dr. Rene Spitz indicated that two- to six-month-olds are satisfied with any face. They will smile freely to a scowling face or to an ugly face mask with its tongue poking back and forth through the mouth slit.

Infants eventually learn that familiar faces are rewarding and unfamiliar ones are poor social risks. Smiling to faces of loved ones rather than to *any* face begins between seventeen to thirty weeks. As you bend over your baby, smiling, talking, and ministering to his needs, you encourage his responsiveness, and smiling becomes associated with pleasure and you. Cooing, smiling back at, picking up, and cuddling babies actually increases smiling. If this rewarding experience stops, infants gradually give up smiling.

An environment can encourage or discourage babies very early. In Israel, Dr. Gewirtz found that most one-month-olds living in nurseries on kibbutzim (collective farms) smiled readily to human faces. In comparison, only one out of five of their institutionalized peers could. The kibbutz infants seemed to be in environments more conducive to learning to smile. In another series of experiments set in the United States, Gewirtz and his team found that reinforcing infant smiles with nods, talk, and smiles, and discouraging crying, frowning, and fussing with expressionless faces made babies very "smiley" indeed.

All this adds up to a crucial point in your baby's life. He is really responding to the feelings and behaviors of others. This is when your value in encouraging or discouraging him clearly emerges.

Feelings are a two-way-street—even with a two-month-old. Your baby clearly influences your behavior, too. Between one and one-half to six months, his smiling controls you. Your baby's laughter, crying, cooing, glances, and stares—and he uses a special variety just for you now—keep you comfortably near while he interacts with you. They encourage new responses from you, feelings you never thought you had.

Smiling and crying communicate important information about the baby's overall well-being which, of course, greatly concerns you. A very young baby is a mystery even to his parents. You have to get to know him. His smiling and crying come close to your responses in similar contexts. They let you identify with your own parent or with yourself as a child. Crying may reflect all kinds of unknown problems that you might have to set right or it may even suggest blame or withdrawal of love. Besides, crying is a high-pitched, loud, lengthy, and very unpleasant kind of sound. Smiling is easily interpreted as appreciation, recognition, and preference for you. It may also preview other interesting and charming events, like calling to or reaching for father. Because most mothers see infant smiles as rewarding, babies biologically predisposed to smile easily and often may elicit more approaches from mother than unsmiling infants who unknowingly might hamper her involvement with them. But you know by now that your baby is an individual even in how much and when he chooses to smile. Even if he does not smile as much as Suzy next door, he needs and wants you all the same.

A Real Character

Smiling, crying, demanding attention—the baby is beginning to register as a personality. If you think about it, there are probably lots of things you can say about him. Here are just two infant personalities.

Baby A

Has an intense drive toward motor performance.

Eats with greed and gusto.

A gulper. He gulps down a bottle with the same vigor he shows in all other areas.

A light sleeper.

Wiry.

A "talker"—terribly interested in communicating with his loved ones.

A ham and an actor.

May be moody. If he becomes overwrought with his body English and gurgles, that charming smile changes with lightning swiftness to frustrated crying.

Has a real temper.

Terribly disinterested in crutches. During the evening fusses. May be fed formula, but shows the same lack of interest in it that he does in his pacifier and same emphatic response (spits it out).

Commands attention with screams or charm—any kind will do.

Despite all this gusto gains 1½ pounds and 1½ inches for a grand total of 11½ pounds and 23 inches.

Baby B

Very quiet.

Relishes eating things he likes (at this stage, his mother's milk).

Eats efficiently, steadily, and neatly.

Sleeps a lot and deeply.

A little bit overweight (13 pounds) for his height but good-looking.

Eyes are his best feature. They are remarkable for their ability to watch and track things and people alertly; even gives up his eating for this.

Especially sensitive to people, does *not* like strangers, and fusses at sitters.

Generally almost too good except for stubbornness.

Finicky and particular. *Very* discriminating about his tastes and quite assertively states some of his preferences. Tastes the first few spoonfuls of a soupy brew you mixed, clenches his mouth shut, frowns, and turns away. Refuses a bottle as emphatically as solids. Strongly prefers one sleep position.

Won't actively seek stimulation, but enjoys it if it is *his* style —gently, please.

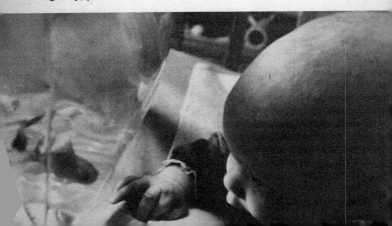

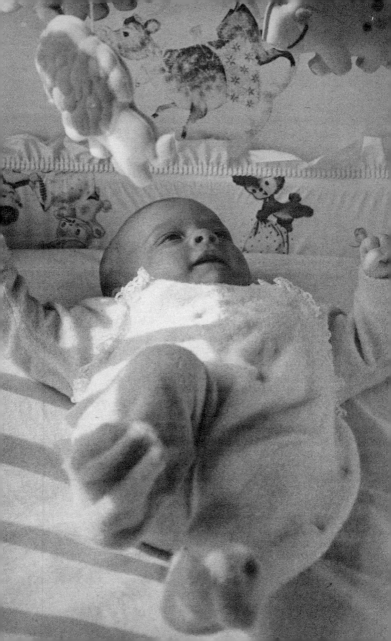

Motor

Large

Startles spontaneously (Moro reflex). Occasional twitches in hands and feet.

Cycles arms and legs smoothly. On tummy, keeps head in mid-position. Can hold head up at 45-degree angle for a few minutes.

When held parallel to ground at torso, tries to hold head up. On back turns head and holds up head recurrently at 45-degree angle.

Sitting

Sitting, keeps head erect, but still bobs.

Small

Grasps becoming voluntary.

Holds object for a few moments; may hold longer.

May swipe at objects.

Language

Active

Small throaty sounds become cooing, vowel-like, but unlike mature human sounds.

Most vocalizing still crying.

Passive

Interested in sounds.

Please do not regard this chart as a rigid timetable. Babies are unpredictable. Some perform an activity earlier or later than the chart indicates.

Growth Chart

Mental

Startles at sounds or shows facial response.

Stares indefinitely at surroundings.

Coordinates eye movements in a circle in regarding light or object. Visually follows them from outer corner of eye past middle of body. Focuses eyes on objects at seven or eight inches. Stares at attractive, large or moving object at several feet.

Moving or contoured objects hold attention longer. Fixates on one of two objects shown.

Reacts with generalized body movements and attempts to grab an attractive object. Retains object briefly as voluntary replaces reflex grasp.

Excites in anticipation of objects, begins to anticipate their movements.

Visually prefers people to objects. Stares at, quiets to face or voice.

Blinks at shadow of his hand. Begins to look at it as object for contemplation. May begin showing preference for right or left side.

Repeats actions for their own sake.

Does one thing at a time.

Clearly discriminates among voices, people, tastes, proximity, and object size. Associates behaviors and people; e.g., mother with meals.

Social

Personal

Shows distress, excitement, delight.

Can quiet self with sucking.

Interaction

Smiles at people, father and sibs besides mother.

Regards person alertly and directly. Excites, orients, moves arms and legs; pants; vocalizes. Visually follows moving person. Begins to prefer three rather than two-dimensional representations of heads.

Quiets to holding, voice, or face. Body tone improves.

Most significant stimulation is still touch and oral, not social.

Stays awake longer if people interact with him. May perform for people.

Cultural

May have only one night feeding.

Moves bowels twice, close to feedings.

Is awake as many as ten hours a day. Has two to four longer sleep periods.
Sleeps as long as seven hours a night.

Enjoys bath.

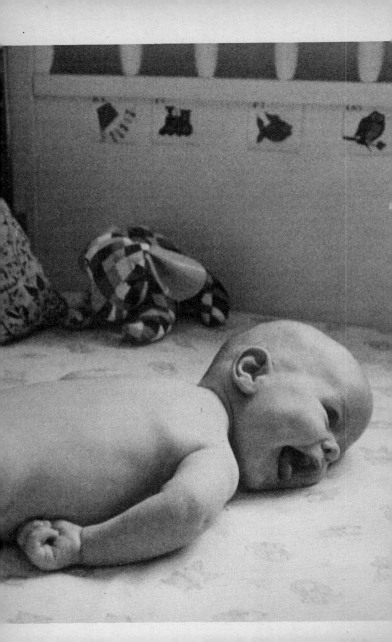

THE
THIRD
MONTH
Getting Ready

THE THIRD MONTH
Getting Ready

The third month of a baby's life is generally easier and more rewarding than the first two—for him and his parents. Almost magically, crying nearly vanishes by the three-month birthday. The baby's increased capacity to engage the world with vocalizing, smiling, facial expressions, and looking at people, his better physical shape and control, and his new reaching ability replace his need to cry. He is an interesting and responsive personality. He can whimper in a special way when he is hungry, chortle as he actively responds to a human being, and squeal with frustration when someone he has been socializing with leaves him. Occasionally he may stop his activity, watch his mother or father, then try a slow gurgle at the back of his throat. Some babies use an expressive face. Your baby may widen his eyes, smack his lips, and grin broadly to a new taste treat. Placed in a position he dislikes, he may stare disgruntled at the guilty party. Since he likes to play and socialize, he smiles immediately and spontaneously with his whole face at someone he recognizes. He may search your face briefly, focus on your mouth and eyes, and become more active, kick his legs, wiggle, and reach with both arms.

Three-month-olds still respond with their whole body to many things and activities. They are still pretty much stuck in their lying-down world and trapped where mothers put them. But they are perceptibly gaining in specialized muscular control. Almost all babies this age can raise their heads while on their tummies and many can hold them up for long periods. This new ability allows them a new, bigger view of their world. Most can keep their bodies compact when picked up and hold up their heads with only a little bobbing when seated. They can sit propped in a lap or a reclining chair and even support themselves independently very briefly. Others when pulled to sit will still flop a little, like rag dolls. Some babies, in fact, can express their feelings very well with "body English." Yours may be able to resist persistent efforts to seat him by firmly arching his back and neck, or let his body sag to protest your interference in an activity such as looking or sucking fingers. He may also arch toward a desirable object with head, face, and open mouth.

All in all, the baby has become so delightful you are very thankful to have him. Your main hope is that you can match his new responsiveness with more of your own—a far cry from the way you felt just two months ago.

Night Owl

You and the baby have solved your first problem, too. His daily patterns of sleeping, eating, and being alert are clearly regulated. He sleeps better and more predictably. He naps quietly for two hours in the morning and an hour and a half in the afternoon. Although bedtime may still be difficult and some infants still sleep only six hours at a stretch, your baby is likely to sleep for ten and occasionally eleven hours by the end of the month.

Even though your baby may still cry with fatigue or suck his fingers as he turns from any new stimulation offered, he can help put himself to sleep with a definite pattern. His preference for his tummy or back is now essential. He wiggles, worms his way into the bedclothes, selects the fingers or things he will stick in his mouth, and sinks in. This nesting activity is often repeated during the night when the baby becomes half-conscious and must drop into deeper sleep again.

His patterns of deep and light sleep, called sleep cycles, are also becoming more predictable, as are his other routines. An active, noisy baby, for example, may be active and noisy even in sleep. Sixty minutes of deep sleep may be sandwiched between light, dreamy and more active states, semi-alert for a total of about three or four hours. Automatically and half-awake, the baby relives and reworks his latest developmental tasks.

He may suck his fingers, rock the crib, bang his head, move about, fuss, coo to himself, cry out, then nestle into his favorite sleep position and down again into deep sleep. These activities, which surface when the baby's state of consciousness allows, use energy left over from the day.

Nighttime might be one period when you can just drop

everything and pick up your baby, especially if you have other children. But your response to his cries and activity will become a necessary part of his getting-myself-back-to-sleep pattern. With your encouragement, the baby may become a real live-wire in the wee hours of the morning, disrupting the rest of the family and alienating you. Allow your baby to establish and use his own return-to-slumber ritual, even if this means occasionally letting him cry himself to sleep.

By the middle of the third month, the baby may begin to eat solids. This is not too soon to establish a comfortable eating exchange with your baby. Since the largest portion of your interaction with him in the earliest weeks is during feeding, some of the baby's important feelings and attitudes toward you will come from it. Coaxing, forcing, silently fuming at him, talking too much with too many people around can make the baby pretty miserable. You do not have to entertain him while you feed him. Eating is enjoyable enough

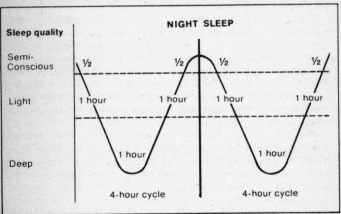

as it is and meals should be happy, pleasant times for you both. Funny as it seems, most things a mother does with her infant, however unrelated in style they may be to each other, are related to her manner of feeding him.

Introducing Solid Foods

You can watch for these clues to your baby's readiness for solids. If he looks around expectantly for something more after his formula or breast feeding, or seems dissatisfied even after as much as eight ounces from a bottle, or thirty minutes at the breast, he is ready. Another clue is the baby's shortening rather than lengthening his nighttime sleep stretches.

Pediatricians suggest that solids be introduced carefully and gradually. Solid feeding before the infant is ready can interfere with breast feeding by filling up the baby or offering too much epicurean variety for him to handle, thus dulling his interest. It also interferes with digestion. The stool analyses of babies under ten weeks have shown "largely undigested particles of complex carbohydrates, fats, and proteins from solid foods." A more mature intestinal tract is better able to digest and react to foods.

Hasty introduction of solids may trigger latent sensitivities to foods. Considering the effort and expense of curing already established allergies, avoiding allergic reactions now is well worth delay and care. To avoid sensitizing your baby, start him on a solid that offers only one challenge at a time, a one-grain cereal like rice, for example. This selection will allow you to identify the offensive agent immediately should your baby demonstrate sensitivity. A mixture of new foods does not allow this important discrimination. Wait a week before adding each new food to allow sensitivity to the preceding one to show itself. Sensitivities can be indicated immediately or more belatedly. A baby may vomit a new food (orange juice is a popular candidate) and continue to every time he is offered it. His stools may be frequent and loose that day or the next. He may be fussy and gassy for several hours. As much as a week later, a dry, scaling rash may appear. If the baby is sensitive to a food, stop it. You may be successful later since allergic reactions become less likely with each successive month.

When you are introducing a solid, give your baby just the tiniest taste, thinned with a little milk so that he has a chance to get used to the new taste and the new consistency gradually. One *baby-sized* bite is enough at first and you can consider you have done well if he takes it. Do not be surprised or discouraged if most of it comes right back out at first. The baby's "rejection" is probably due to novelty. Suddenly he must eat new food with new tools, and it has to be swallowed instead of sucked down. Baby's first attempts at *conscious* swallowing, which start around his tenth to twelfth week, are labored. Like many conversions from reflex to voluntary behavior, mastery of this new way to get food down involves a delay. Even after your baby has learned to swallow voluntarily, he may show you that he still favors his first swallowing and sucking by sucking his hands or fingers between spoonfuls. These are not his real "I've-had-enough" clues, however. When he simply cannot swallow efficiently anymore, he will signal your quitting time by spitting out more than you spoon in. To avoid these complications, some mothers put loose solids in bottles and use nipples with large holes to let the baby "drink" the food. Such a gimmick only delays learning to swallow. One value in using a spoon is its help in teaching your baby a new and necessary way to eat.

If your baby repeatedly balks and chokes on a new food, try tasting it first to see if it *is* all right. If he continues to refuse what you find wholesome, you should try another taste treat, a sweeter food, like applesauce or any mashed fruit. Otherwise he will get into the habit of turning you down. Wait a few days, then try the previous food again. Your baby may surprise you by liking it the second time around.

After solids are started, some babies may stop eating almost entirely for several meals. Then they may eat for days as if they can hardly get enough, only to drop back and level off again. On the other hand, some babies like solids so much that they refuse milk. Since a baby this age needs milk far more than solids for nourishment, try giving him his milk first and limiting his solids. For most babies, two tablespoons of a particular solid are enough and will allow for needed milk intake.

Do not get too uptight about the feeding exchange. Because you and your baby are getting to know each other over the first few months, your feelings and affection for him are far more important to him than the absolute amount of time you spend with him now or your particular style of feeding and physical contact. One single child-rearing practice is very unlikely to be decisive for your child's personality development.

Immunization

Dr. Frank Falkner, professor of pediatrics at the University of Cincinnati, believes however that there *is* an optimal immunization procedure for babies, and there are good reasons for this.

The average newborn arrives in this world already partially immunized by the mother. He has two kinds of natural immunity from the fetal stage—antibodies against certain diseases, like diptheria and/or allergies of dust and pollen or protein found in cow's milk. A natural way to encourage this natural immunity is breast feeding. This is why pediatricians urge mothers to breast feed if at all possible. This kind of protection could be lifelong.

However, some of the natural immunities against diseases and allergies are not very lasting. Pediatricians, therefore, advocate a regime of innoculations—often more painful for the mother than baby.

The immunization routine that Dr. Falkner considers optimal looks like this:

Baby's Age	Name of Innoculation	Name of Disease to be Resisted
2 Months	DTP	Diptheria, Tetanus, Pertussis (Whooping Cough)
	Oral Polio Vaccine	Polio
4 Months	DTP	
	Oral Polio Vaccine	
6 Months	DTP	
12 Months	Tuberculin Test	
15 Months	Measles Rubella (German measles) Mumps	
18 Months	DTP Oral Polio Vaccine	

Twenty years ago, the innoculation program for many American babies looked like this:

Baby's Age	Name of Innoculation
One day	Smallpox
	Tuberculin
6 Months	DTP
7 Months	DTP
9 Months	DTP

Hand Play

When he is awake and alert after feedings, watch your baby learning and playing as he carefully explores facets of light, colors, shapes, patterns, sounds. He can play for longer periods now, up to three-quarters of an hour at a time. He already recognizes and attends to your sounds in the distance. He even stops his sucking to listen. He watches a face or follows the objects on his mobile as if they were a new experience each time. When your face appears, he calms quickly and he may concentrate on it intensely. As he stares, he seems to arch his head to reach for you with his eyes and his mouth forms a circle. He shifts his attention to each new object on his mobile and as it moves, he follows it with his eyes. He can concentrate on a picture at the side of his crib or on a toy in the distance. At birth he can focus only on objects and people eight inches away from his eyes. His focal capacity extends with each month until by his third month he can see objects all over a room.

Some infants are acutely sensitive to the outside world and invest much more heavily in these watching, listening, and touching activities than in physical practice. This kind of baby may be slower to grasp an object placed in his hand, but more acute in sensing each new aspect of it as he turns it in different directions. He will stroke his cheek with it and bring it to his mouth for further exploration while a more active baby would throw it out of his crib. Since large motor milestones are the most common measure in the United States for estimating a child's developmental progress, a baby like this may seem dull when he is really perfecting much more complicated skills.

One of the most important bits of early play that you will see involves something as simple as your baby looking at and playing with his hands. Hand-to-mouth organization, which begins as a reflex, is the first step in this process. As the baby brings his hand to his mouth, he begins to sense the gratifying stimulation at each end of this circuit. He brings a toy in his hand to his mouth, grasps things placed in his mouth, and so begins to appreciate the touch, feel, and taste of the things around him. Hand regard and play follow. The baby holds his hand before him and adds seeing to the circuit. One of the reasons he does this is that his eyes can work together now to focus on objects like his hands. Simply looking at his hands seems to prompt the activity, and he plays with them for long periods. He watches his fingers move slowly, catching light, and at times intertwines his newly found toys. He looks back and forth between his hands, brings them together, giggles, and grins as they clutch each other. Then he pulls his arms apart and snaps his fingers away.

He seems pleased with combining the feelings of their motion and watching them as they move. He often explores his face with his hand, and as it reaches his mouth, still the ultimate goal of exploration, his fingers slide in and he begins to suck them. He circles his feet in front of his eyes for long periods, and in the same visual space his jingly mobile appears. The first time his whirling arms make it jingle and move, he sobers, concentrates, and gingerly bats it again. His efforts to whirl and move it become more deliberate. He remembers his behavior for he pursues his previous efforts religiously when he is wide awake and comfortable in his crib.

Your baby will also begin reaching out to each side for an object. If you hold a toy over him, his arms wave in circles at his sides at the sight of it. Gradually they come together to meet, grasp, and hold it. His grasp of the toy may still be automatic, but he holds onto it now voluntarily. Bit by bit, with practice, his grasp will become more systematic, more selective, and smoother. He may wave the object, although a baby less interested in physical activity will do this at around four months of age. Things a three-month-old sees become exercise material for his hands. He has learned that objects can be transformed by his own activity.

This kind of play has many dimensions. The baby's hand activity is self-instruction in depth perception, as well as in manipulating distance, appearance, and size. A three-month-old will move his arms more when a toy such as a shiny ball is close to him than when it is far away and unattainable.

The determined repetition that the baby shows in batting his mobile helps, too, in the growth of memory. The more an act is performed, the more likely it is to be remembered and a memory trace is established in the brain. The baby's memory from one day to the next makes daily relearning unnecessary. He can then add a new piece of behavior each time to his already learned repertoire of activities.

Continuity and Trust

He will reveal his developing memory in yet another way. He is learning to wait for an expected reward such as a feeding. Even if he cries about a slight delay, he may stop as soon as he hears your footsteps and lie in his crib expectantly as you prepare to feed him. When you pick him up to change him before the feeding, he looks serious and attentive but doesn't cry.

Since his new accomplishment is still fragile, your consistency in repeating the steps of the sequence is important. Even leaving him for a moment strapped to the changing table may "blow his cool." Unable to contain himself any longer, he wails with disappointment. Continuity of care, according to Dr. Anna Freud, is one of the three most important elements in a child's development, the others being affection and a stimulating environment. Young babies actually seem to enjoy repetition of an action or experience. At least in early infancy, a baby who is gratified much of the time and experiences a minimum of frustration can handle stress far better than a baby subjected to frequent tension or disruption of routine.

Loss of predictability in his environment, in the timing of patterns, and in styles of gratification can distress a very young baby as much as the loss of a loved one. In fact, unpredictability works against the very thing you may ultimately want for your child: sturdy self-sufficiency. Parents who sometimes encourage and sometimes fail to respond to their child's early dependency actually encourage his fragility. The need for some background of events one can count on is essential even to adults. If you are easily distracted from what you have led your baby to expect, his ability to build trust in his environment will suffer.

Obviously a perfect relationship where mother always comes through promptly with the "right" response is impossible. There will be times, too, when your baby cries just to let off tension and energy. But the degree of your consistency in answering your baby's signals is important. When a mother's responses to her baby's needs are usually prompt and appropriate, she builds an important idea. He begins to believe and expect that his behavior, tiny as he is, influences his environment. How differently an infant must feel when no one responds to his wails—either because mother is too busy with other children or does not care enough, or because he is in an institution where dozens of babies are bidding for their parcels of attention. By the time someone does manage to come, his limited memory just does not allow him to recall that his cry brought about the attention. This belief in the value of your own actions is vital later on; in intelligence and personality tests, it has been repeatedly related to achievement, behavior and learning.

Discovering His Capacities

Your baby may be just beginning to associate a few of his actions with their results—a big step in learning. The hand-to-mouth organization already mentioned is one of the first examples of an activity style that still features total body commitment to an activity. As the baby brings his hand to mouth, he begins to sense the gratifying stimulation at each end of this mouth-hand circuit just as he begins to realize that swiping at a toy dangling above him can make it move and jingle. He is beginning to learn cause-and-effect.

The baby's glimmering awareness that his hands and feet are extensions of *himself* is part of his awareness of himself and his difference from the world. He is learning about their extending, reaching capacities, just as he is learning his possibilities, limitations, and compensations for limitations. His whimpering for a change of pace when bouncing and vocalizing wear him out signals his understanding that he cannot handle a slow-down himself as well as he could with someone else's help. His waiting for you to give him back a toy that he has dropped means he is beginning to realize his limits in reproducing certain activities, as well as your role in helping him compensate for his inability.

Hand regard and play are also part of the baby's growing ability to reach out and grab things in his environment. It starts with the tonic neck reflex, which automatically raises the baby's arm on the same side to which his head and eyes are turned. Bringing his hand into direct view, which usually happens at around two months, is the first step toward the baby's visual control of his hands. Possibly his improved vision has something to do with this timing. He can blink at will, as well as automatically, and his ability to see things at different distances improves dramatically. One development multiplies the other. When the baby differentiates his hands as objects for contemplation, his ability to pay attention for longer periods in his day jumps abruptly.

One-armed swiping at objects rapidly follows, usually with a closed fist. As the grasp reflex fades, the baby's fingers are freer to move, touch, and grasp one another. Eventually, the baby's hands will be able to meet over his chest or tummy. As the baby accumulates experience at fisted swiping, the movement will become more controlled, a slow approach of the hand to the object, sometimes accompanied by glances between hand and object and completed with a fumbling grasp. About the fifth month, the baby will be able to move his hand rapidly from outside his visual field to grasp an object directly and smoothly.

Internalizing Information

Despite the baby's efforts to swipe at objects and hold up his head, you may feel that he is far less active than he was during his first month. Remember that appearances are deceiving. Some fantastic things happen inside your baby about this stage in his life.

In some recent research at the Educational Testing Service in Princeton, New Jersey, Dr. Michael Lewis found that three-month-olds have an image of the human face in mind. Three-month-olds at the Infant Laboratory differentiated pictures of normal and abnormal faces. The babies smiled more to a normal face than to a cyclops, though they stared at both the same amount of time. Dr. Lewis has also shown repeatedly that babies older than three months have a short-term memory. Infants over two months of age become bored with repeated visual signals, but younger infants do not. A baby has to remember a signal to become bored with its repetition. This difference in memory suggests a major mental overhaul around three months of age.

Hanus Papousek, a noted Czechoslovakian psychologist, has noted an abrupt increase in reaction and a "marked, qualitative change in higher nervous function" at the beginning of the third month of life. He reports that in the first two months, infants followed from birth showed qualitative changes only in general body activity and vocalizing. From the eleventh week of life, however, they reacted more specifically and more appropriately to the experimental situation. Their vocal and facial reactions were like those of an adult, showing joy, indecision, uncertainty, and pleasure. Hand movements with toys were visually absent in the first six weeks, occurred in 30 percent of the observation periods from eight to ten weeks, and then abruptly and significantly increased to 60 percent on the twelfth week. After the twelfth week, these movements again increased very slowly.

In your home, you can see signs of your baby's increasing mental competence if you look for them. By now, he may recognize you, other family members, even a few familiar objects. When he sees his bottle, he may brighten, arch forward, open his eyes and mouth, and wave both hands. In contrast to his smile for father, which he accompanies with more activity, he melts all over for you and smiles, crinkling his eyes and face. Your baby may also know what to do when he wants you to respond to him. You may see him search for you when you are reading or working in the same room. As he finds you, he coos until you return his glance, then fusses for you to come. When he wants you to pick him up from his chair, he arches forward as he looks at you.

When you enter the nursery, he startles and whimpers for you to come to him.

Electronic machine print-outs of babies' brain waves support mothers' observations and experimental reports. They show marked changes in activity and rhythms after three months of age. For the first time, baby's brain waves approximate those of an adult. The chemical balance and cell composition of the brain has also changed dramatically. Primitive reflexes disappear or begin to disappear at this time, signaling that a higher level of the brain is assuming control. During his first three months, most of a baby's behavior is beyond his control. His body simply responds automatically to certain kinds of stimulation. Now the tonic neck, swimming, walking, grasping, and swallowing reflexes start losing their hold on the baby's behavior. During the shift from reflex to willed muscular control, body areas governed by brain regions where transitions are occurring may be less active than before or after. Since neither the "higher" nor "lower" brain is working for the baby's benefit, the switchover means temporary disorganization. That is why a three-month-old baby will move his legs less than he did as a newborn. His quietness is only "momentary." Once a major reflex like the tonic neck reaction fades, arms and legs are free to move together instead of one-sidedly and the baby will twist to one side and flip over less often. These signs alone should reassure you that your baby is getting ready for the serious job of engaging and moving about in his world.

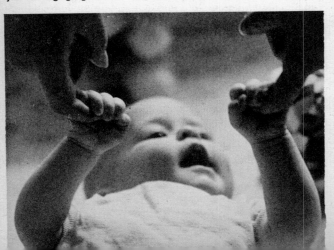

The Importance of Stimulation

1928

There is a sensible way of treating children. Treat them as though they were young adults. Dress them, bathe them with care and circumspection. Let your behavior always be objective and kindly firm. Never hug and kiss them, never let them sit in your lap. If you must kiss them once on the forehead (to) say goodnight.... Try it out. In a week's time you will find how easy it is to be perfectly objective with your child and at the same time kindly. You will be utterly ashamed of the mawkish, sentimental way you have been handling it.

from *Psychological Care of Infant and Child* by J. B. Watson

1967

The evidence suggests that giving a young baby what he seems to be seeking in the way of stimulation and gratification will make him well disposed toward his environment ... It takes so little in material outlay to give a small baby a full life. What he needs from adults, outside of physical care, is sensitivity to the cues he offers, freedom to do what he is capable of, and the good sense to stop short of over-stimulating him. If all this sounds like making a baby under six months the household kingpin, consider his inevitable frustrations—wet diapers, swallowed air, delayed feedings, occasional bumps, chafed skin, new foods that don't agree, prickling shots and prodding medical examination. Consider too—what is more pleasant for a baby's caretakers than seeing him enjoying life and making the most of it?

from *Early Childhood: Behavior and Learning* by Catherine Landreth

All this increased and more personalized responsiveness from your baby requires more sophisticated stimulation from mother and father. Since you are more confident, more familiar, and more attached to him by now, this should not be too hard. So much of what your baby has already accomplished has been activated or initiated by you—his parents. You are his providers, stimulators, shock absorbers, and teachers. You gratify his needs and adapt his environment for him—sometimes protecting him from it, sometimes organizing it differently, and occasionally exposing him more directly.

We have only recently begun to learn from psychologists, physicians, educators, and their colleagues how much the amount and kind of stimulation from the environment influences a child's development. Babies whose parents handle, play with, imitate, smile, and talk to them, who provide things for them to look at, listen to, and explore with their mouths and hands are advanced in attentiveness, visual pursuit, and coordinated movements, and tend to carry their early advantage over into later life.

Dr. Leon Yarrow, Chief of the Social and Behavioral Sciences Branch of the National Institute of Child Health and Human Development, says: "Perhaps the most striking finding is the extent to which developmental progress during the first six months appears to be influenced by maternal stimulation. The amount and quality of stimulation are highly related to I.Q. These data suggest that mothers who give much and intense stimulation and encouragement to practice developmental skills tend to be successful in producing infants who make rapid developmental progress." He adds that "appropriateness of the stimulation to the child's individual and developmental characteristics," as well as gratification of his needs and mother's affectionate exchange also help mental development.

Like a shock absorber, the mother protects her child from too much stimulation from inside himself (like hunger or pain) or from the outside world (like cold or noise). She also enhances the positive aspects of her baby's world and directs his attention to them. Mother's sensitivity and capability in adapting the environment to her baby's characteristics actually boosts his ability to handle stress. Since he is completely dependent on you, he will need you to get him out of the binds he gets himself into and to help and protect him in periods of rage and frustration. If he propels himself to the top of his crib and wedges himself into a corner, come to the rescue and pull him to the center, even though you know he will just start all over and scream for help again. If you respond to his needs, you will enhance his and your pleasure with his learning and practice. Leaving him to his own devices may make him so fearful of situations he cannot escape from that he "turns off." You can also show him ways to extract himself from his frenzy and his predicament. After a few reruns, he will know how to turn around and get out of that corner.

If your baby is lucky, you will spend a lot of your day watching him perform and actively play with and enjoy him. When you comfort, cuddle or rock him, he relaxes, quiets, and looks intently into your face. Not only is he stimulated visually, the whole tone of his body improves as he responds to your physical warmth and presence. A parent should try to see that her baby gets enough stimulation of his developing senses—enough sucking, looking, touching, listening—to give him practice so he can move to more complex behavior. The more stimulation he has a chance to get used to, the less easily will he be upset by new sights, sounds, and feelings. Infants are more sturdy and responsive than formerly believed. If you give yours enough to look at and to listen to, he will begin to be able to take much more.

Developing the important ability to pay attention does not just come with age. It depends on experience, too. Dr. Michael Lewis has shown that during a baby's first year of life, babying, protectiveness, affection, approval, the amount a mother smiles, touches, and talks to her baby and, very importantly, the promptness and appropriateness of her response to the baby's crying and other signals—all relate to his greater responsiveness. The more attentive the baby, the higher his mental capacity at three and one-half years of age, as measured by the Stanford-Binet Tests of Intelligence. A baby who gets this stimulation also tends to be more responsive to his mother, less irritable, and more interested in exploring his environment and rehearsing his skills as they unfold in their developmental sequences. As the baby explores his environment, the number of activities that interest him increases. Dr. Jerome Bruner says: "The more a baby sees, the more he wants to see." He is building a vocabulary of sense experiences and forming abilities on which later learning depends: paying attention and developing specific, controlled sequences of actions. Practice in looking and touching things enables him to differentiate these activities from the rest of his behavior and then relate them to each other usefully until eventually he can reach out and take hold of something he sees. For the infant to learn from experience, he must have experience to learn from. Early perceptual experience prepares a baby for the later development of coordinated, visually directed behavior, which Dr. Robert L. Fantz says "is essential to active exploration and manipulation of the environment."

Lack of stimulation is devastating to the growing infant. His emotional growth needs encouragement and stimulation as much as his physiological growth needs proper food and rest. Saying that a crying baby "just wants attention" makes as much sense as saying "He just wants food." They are both real needs. Feed him if he is hungry, and if he is bored do not let him "cry it out." Try picking him up and bringing him into the family circle where he can enjoy its richness.

Even if it is not always exactly appropriate, a baby can handle and assimilate such stimulation. Referring to the need for providing infants with "a rich, varied, and appropriate sensory environment," Dr. Nahman H. Greenberg, research director of the University of Illinois' Child Development Clinic, says, "If, in his early weeks, the infant's environment fails to provide the conditions that bring about the fulfillment of sensory needs, the effect may be great. In later weeks or months, the infant with lowered thresholds and hypersensitization may react severely when subjected to the usual amounts and kinds of stimuli."

Since the baby spends a lot of time lying flat on his back or tummy, head to the side, hanging toys on the sides rather than over the crib is a good idea. An encounter with an "interesting" or novel sight can stimulate a baby to pay attention and can even keep a drowsy baby awake for as long as half an hour. No one suggests subjecting your baby to a ceaseless barrage of stimulation from which he cannot escape. Too much handling and anxious stimulation may create reactions like excessive crying, tension, irritability, even "colic." A baby needs quiet times, too. Just as there is no one way to love a baby, there is no one way to stimulate him. The challenge and the pleasure lie in finding the ways and the amounts that are right for your baby and you. Sometimes the same stimulation can arouse or quiet a baby depending on his state of being. Babies differ in their styles of refusing stimulation. One baby may actively move to refuse objectionable stimulation while another's body may sag in protest until he feels like a sack of meal. They differ also in their ability to signal a need for stimulation. Babies who demand attention for themselves are easier to read. Overtures for attention and affection may not come from a quiet baby.

Babies are unalike in their sensitivity and responses to excitation and the degree of it they can stand. Infants who work hard at learning an activity may be somewhat insensitive and inflexible. You may find breaking into long play or practice sessions difficult. The baby fusses or protests until you allow him to continue. This determination reflects his serious investment in a task, which leaves him relatively insensitive to surrounding distraction. You can turn this quality into a learning asset. If you need to switch him to another activity, make the transition for him instead of frustrating him and yourself. Distract him, for example, with a toy. As you draw his interest from physical activity to watching the toy, he will be readier for another kind of play or for the necessities such as sleeping and feeding. The disadvantages of leaving the baby to his self-assigned learning tasks are that they limit him. He learns new activities from the novel stimulation you feed him.

Some babies need and enjoy gentler stimulation. A quiet baby's first surprise smile may excite you so much that you try to draw him out more. Instead of blossoming, he may become serious or turn away to look at an object or one of his hands. A gentler approach might be better. "Play with your baby whenever you want to" is obviously an inadequate guideline for this kind of sensitive infant. His delayed, slow responses to stimulation and his gentleness demand a special kind and limited range of stimulation. Outside this range, he may not respond.

Besides sensitivity, persistence may be needed to stimulate an inactive baby. Sometimes fears of making mistakes, "disturbing" or hurting him deter parents. Or a mother's overprotectiveness discourages a father's more active play. The muscular relaxation that often characterizes a quiet baby is an added deterrent. Yet leaving him in his crib or infant chair much of his day, undisturbed except by a smooth pattern of sleeping and eating, will only make a quiet baby quieter. You will help prevent his isolation if you continue to reach out to him.

Such a baby's even disposition, which remains unruffled by any of the usual events of an infant's day, may be the most difficult aspect for the mother, especially if she herself is expressive and energetic. Such a baby may not even mind his mother's forgetting to feed him at the appropriate time. This quiet, slow, or virtually nonexistent response to stimulation is known as poor "feedback." It is dramatic in babies with neurological defects, deafness, or blindness, but also occurs in physically and mentally normal babies, both boys and girls.

When a mother has to give so much of herself to a new baby, she instinctively expects a rewarding, cuddly dependence. Failure to get a rewarding response may make her avoid playing with her baby, question her and her baby's adequacy, or feel depressed and weary. This denial sets up a vicious circle—the mother's withdrawal and lack of stimulation further depress the infant, who responds even less and discourages his mother even more. A mother need not feel that she alone is responsible for difficult communication between her and her baby. The baby's sex and personality, to which he is already predisposed upon entry into this world, influence the exchange as much as the mother's personality. Mothers stimulate baby boys more than girls during the first few months of life, possibly because boys sleep less and cry more than girls. Yet research shows that mothers imitate and verbalize with their baby girls more than their boys. Many mothers do perfectly well with a certain kind of baby and less well with another. The same mother may handle a gentle baby girl with great warmth and sensitivity, while she may be utterly thwarted by a tense, driving, demanding baby boy.

To break the communication gap, look for things the baby especially likes. If he is quiet and contained, visual delights may be his "bag." Not every child has to be the all-American athlete. A fussy baby quiets when given things to look at or listen to. Unless he is very hungry, he usually will have longer quiet periods, and cry less if he is given toys in his crib, or held up and carried around so he can see what is going on. Once you do reach him, your baby will gather energy. You will find that the communication cycle will generate more and more reward for each of you in the exciting and definitely more active months ahead.

During the past three months, your baby has selectively explored his world through the only channels he has had— his senses of taste, touch, smell, sight, and sound. He has prepared himself for later explorations, manipulation and control of the environment, and has established a base for another kind of contact with it, active physical participation.

Motor

Large

Switches from reflex to voluntary body control. Tonic neck reflex disappearing.

On back, keeps head in midposition and posture symmetrical, lifts head. Moves arm and leg on one side of body in unison, then the other side. Or arms together, legs together. Moves arms and turns head vigorously. When picked up, brings body up compactly.

On tummy, holds chest up and head erect for about ten seconds; may lift head for many minutes.

Lies on tummy with hips low, legs flexed.

When pulled to stand, presses feet against surface and stands briefly.

Sitting

Sits supported. Can help maintain position. Minimum head bobbing.

Small

Keeps hands predominantly open, grasp reflex fading.
May be unable to grasp object.

Begins to swipe, but may be far off target.
Reaches for object with both arms, starting at sides and closing in front of body, often contacts object with closed fists.

Language

Active

Cooing one syllable, vowel-like sounds—ooh, ah, ae.
Whimpers, chortles, gurgles at back of throat, squeals, chuckles.

Cries less.

Vocalizes relatively independently of environment.
Vocal-social response; e.g., to mother's smile and talk.

Passive

Listens to voices.
Distinguishes speech sounds.
Perceives syllable unit.

Please do not regard this chart as a rigid timetable. Babies are unpredictable. Some perform an activity earlier or later than the chart indicates.

Growth Chart

Mental

Attentive up to three quarters of an hour at a time.

Follows an object with eyes and head from side to side of body for at least ten seconds as it is slowly moved about a few feet in front of face. Responds facially to object. Concentrates on picture or toy close-up or in distance.

Glances from one object to another. Regards dangling object at middle of body promptly.
Swipes with closed fist or reaches with two hands for it.
Glances at rattle in hand.
Retains object in hand voluntarily. Manipulates ring; simple play with rattle.

Distinguishes near and distant objects in space. Experiments with changes in proximity by drawing in and extending arm.

Begins to show memory. Waits for expected reward like a feeding.

Becomes bored with repeated sounds or images.

Quickly calms to concentrate on a face. Attends more to three- than two-dimensional faces. Begins to recognize and differentiate family members.

Watches hands and feet at length. Combines sensations of movement and looking. Explores face, eyes, mouth with hand. Begins to become aware of self.

Tries to prolong pleasing image or action by continuing to look, listen, or grasp. Repeats actions for their own sake. May associate action with result.

Stops sucking to listen. Looks and sucks at the same time.

Searches with eyes for a sound.

Responds to most kinds of stimulation and effort with total body. Switches over to control by "higher brain." Swallowing and grasping become voluntary. Begins to integrate voluntary and reflex behaviors.

Social

Personal

Begins to sense that hands and feet are extensions of himself with limits and possibilities.

Interaction

Smiles immediately and spontaneously.
Crying decreases dramatically.
Expressive alternatives with face, body tone, and vocalizing increase.
Chortles, squeals with frustration, whimpers with hunger, smacks lips.
Visually recognizes mother.

Responds with total body to face he recognizes.

When held, arms and legs push quietly.

Orients and signals distinctively to each of several people. May stop or start crying according to who holds him. Cries differently when mother leaves versus other people. Smiles, vocalizes, orients differently to mother's presence or voice. Tries to attract her attention.

Turns head to speaking or singing voices, familiar person's sounds, an approaching adult.

Social stimulation becomes more important.
Vocalizes when talked to.

Cultural

Patterns of eating, being alert, and sleeping clearly regulated.
One night feeding.
Ready for solids.

Two naps, a couple of hours in morning and a couple in the afternoon.
Sleeps about ten hours a night.

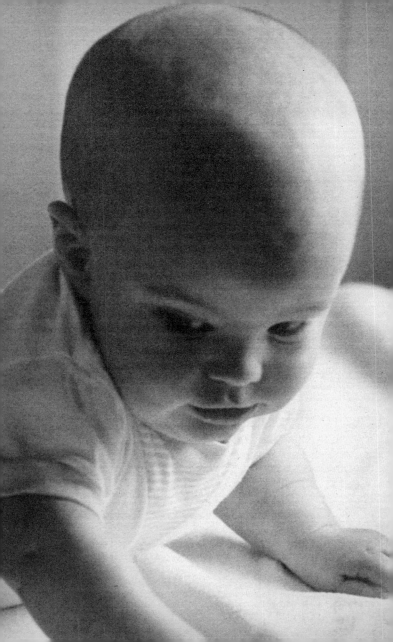

THE
FOURTH
MONTH
A Visionary

THE FOURTH MONTH
A Visionary

By four months of age, babies and their families shape up. As you cuddle your baby now you will probably find his body strong, firm, well padded, but not fat—and it "stays together." His elbows and knees are dimpled. His skin is smooth, spotless, and minus its newborn "fur," which doctors call lanugo. Rashes are short term when they come. Two lower front teeth may be coming in. The baby is fun to be with—not only because of his good looks, but also because of his responsiveness and obvious delight in being held, bounced, cuddled, sat up, and played with. The three to six minutes of responsiveness after feedings in the first month have stretched to as much as three-quarters of an hour. Feeding periods themselves are more enjoyable though a bit messy. The baby is more cooperative and interested. Besides his milk, he consumes as much as half a jar each of two baby foods. Solids are clearly "in." He has also established a definite interval between feeding and eliminations. By now, even less adaptable babies have stopped the late night feeding themselves. Most can probably give up the 10 P.M. feeding, too, although you yourself may still want that chance for closeness with your baby, especially if other children prevent peaceful daytime feedings.

If you do want the baby to adjust to three meals and three milk feedings instead of four, you can help him make the transition with the following schedule:

7 A.M.: Milk
8:30–9 A.M.: Cereal and fruit
12–1 P.M.: Milk, meat, vegetables
5 P.M.: Cereal and fruit
6:30 P.M.: Milk

Deferring the two ends of the day to 7 A.M. and 6:30 P.M. teaches the baby to span the periods between meals longer than four hours apart. As he gets used to three milk feedings, the first two meals at 7 and 8:30 A.M. can be combined, as can the last two meals at 5 and 6:30 P.M. so that the baby may eat, for example, at 7 A.M., noon, and 6 P.M.

Eating Is Play

Feeding sessions are opportunities for socializing. If you talk to him during feedings, his cooing, gurgling, and vocalizing will last for as long as thirty minutes before he returns to breast or bottle to finish. A social animal with none of our social conventions, the baby relishes his role as the sloppy prince. He always has sucked his fingers after a bite, but now he may try his entire first, or prefer to play with his father's hands when he is feeding him. His delicate licking of lips and fingers does not quite clean his hand enough to prevent its smearing his face. He is so anxious to "talk," look at his family in action, or play with your clothes, hair, or face that he sucks in short bursts or stops entirely, milk drooling down his cheeks and chin. Although drooling, finger-sucking, exploration of his mouth with his hand, shortened interest in the breast or bottle may indicate teething, they are all a part of the baby's increasing interest in the world.

The baby's reduction of nursing time in favor of people-watching is no problem for him. If he is breast feeding, he may be able to take what he needs—four to six ounces—from the breasts in the first five minutes. But you may have a problem. Stimulation to the breasts, cut abruptly, can decrease milk supply. If this happens, more frequent nursing will bring it back. Another help might be morning and evening feedings in a dark, quiet room with no distractions. Your baby should suck for the usual period and your milk will return. You might also try this if shortening a feeding is necessary or your baby is not eating enough.

Despite the baby's distractability and the "inconveniences," feeding times with the family should be retained whenever possible for they are among your baby's most valuable socializing periods. After all, this delightful, dynamic creature is well worth the effort. Dr. Leon Yarrow of the National Institute of Health says a baby who lives during the first six months in an environment charged with frequent, exuberant expressions of good feelings and lots of face-to-face socializing with loved ones will have far more than the normal share of social initiative and get-up-and-go.

The family itself often shares moments of quiet and content, much to its collective amazement. Father is no longer listening with one ear cocked for the latest domestic catastrophe. You are beginning to feel rested and together again after a night's sleep or one of the baby's long naps. Baby's brothers and sisters, if he has them, have adjusted and are beginning to cope with their feelings about him. You can let toddlers bring diapers, toys, baby food. Let them hold the baby briefly under your surveillance. School-aged youngsters can really help you to feed, bathe and change the baby.

The baby is doing more things, too, and he has really begun to explore the outside world. He can reach for, grab, carry toward him, and let go of toys—and the whole routine automatically requires bringing the thing to his mouth for sampling. Through such activities he is establishing links between the realms of self and environment.

The more agile and varied use of his hands and his widening interest in things around him also contribute to more finger-sucking and exploration of his face and mouth. A study utilizing charts kept by mother-observers showed that extra-nutritional sucking occupied as much as four hours of a four-month-old's day.

The baby can be pulled to sit and holds his head steady when he gets there. Seated or lying on his tummy, he can turn his head and look in all directions. On his tummy, he can push up on straight arms and bring his head up to a 90-degree angle. He may arch his back, spread his arms and legs out stiffly like an airplane, and seesaw. He can roll over from his back to his side and sometimes all the way over to his tummy—which gives him new vistas to look at and automatically stretches his attention span.

After some practice, a precocious four-month-old may also be pulled to stand, maintaining his weight briefly. While only reflex stiffening, standing delights him and makes him aware of the act itself. If your baby is very active, he may enjoy standing so much that it stops his crying and makes him bypass a sitting position in favor of going all the way up. To get him to sit, you may actually have to bend him at the waist.

This is also the time to keep one hand *firmly* on your whirling dervish whenever you turn your back. Even if your baby is not the most rambunctious, he can slither from under a casually placed hand. He is much too active and interested in the world beyond to leave on any height. He can flip off a changing table quicker than you can move. He can work his way to the edge of a bed and drop off. If you have to leave him, strap him or put him on the floor, where he will be a lot safer.

One by one, the baby will combine the motor achievements of supported sitting, arching his back, head-turning, and looking parallel to the surface on which he sits or lies to yield a marvelously new, three-dimensional space that he can make or change by himself.

Seeing Is Believing

A four-month-old is fully able to delight visually in this new world. His eyesight is reaching adult standards. Unlike many infants in the animal kingdom, human infants are born able to see. Research has indicated that they can discriminate some colors at two weeks and they definitely respond to brightness values in the first month. A newborn prefers patterns to solids. His eyes and brain are developed enough to perceive form. He is aware of movement, probably the earliest, most basic perception. A baby glances at moving objects his very first day on earth and may follow a moving light within the first few hours.

But newborn vision *is* limited. Many things make up visual ability—the ability of the eye to see color, adjust itself to different distances, to see one image instead of double, to orient to moving objects, and to perceive depth. All these visual abilities mature and start working together around the fourth month. The reasons are not yet fully understood. For example, how the brain and eye process color information, as well as the development of the baby's processing ability, still remain mysterious. Somehow by the fourth month, babies clearly see the world in technicolor. They discriminate the colors of the spectrum and even have preferences. They look longer at red and blue than gray, for example.

The eye can also see things farther away. In comparison to the seven-inch to eight-inch object distance a newborn handles, a two-month-old can follow a moving object *at least* several feet away. Studies on vision indicate that a two-month-old cannot follow a moving object at six or eight feet.

By the fourth month, the baby coordinates his eye and head rotations about as well as an adult who wants to follow an object with his eyes. The baby's head participates more and more strongly in tracking an object rotating around him and he can orient himself toward the object of his attention. In addition, babies this age, like adults, use two different styles of head and eye rotation. When the *baby* chooses to direct his gaze to something, his head movements lead his eyes. When changes in the *object* compel his attention, the faster eye system leads the head. In either case, the eye and head move toward the middle of the body, probably because the eyes have to be centered to guide the baby's hands on either side of it.

Although scientists have not discovered as much about other senses as they have about these aspects of sight, available findings indicate that the baby also develops adequate hearing, taste, and smell around the same stage of life. What scientists really want to know, says Dr. Robert L. Fantz of Western Reserve University, is "when and under what circumstances the infant's visual experience yields useful knowledge of the environment." They already have a few answers for us. Your baby's ability to see his hands at different distances helps him reach accurately for things. Studies on baby animals show that a kitten's or a puppy's inability to watch its limbs as it uses them severely impairs physical development. In a now-famous experiment, Dr. Eleanor Gibson had six-and-one-half- to twelve-month-old babies crawl over a large sheet of strong glass supported by a wooden frame. A textured pattern was directly under one half of the glass. Under the other half, the same pattern appeared at a greater depth. Despite enticing toys and the entreaties of their mothers—both at the side that looked deeper—the babies steadfastly refused to cross the "deep" side although they crawled readily over the shallow. Independent of environmental reward or punishment, they were using their information about depth to what they felt was their own advantage.

For a long time Dr. Gibson's experiment established a bottom limit. Perception of depth develops at least as soon as locomotion is possible. But her experiment was limited by the infant's crawling competence. Babies had to crawl to prove that they could see differences in depth and process the information usefully.

In another ingenious experiment, Dr. Roger Webb, formerly of Harvard's Center for Cognitive Studies, indicated that *three*-month-olds see differences in depth and act on the information. When red and silver balls appeared suddenly from behind screens a foot away, the heartbeat and movements of seated three- and four-month-olds increased dramatically in preparation for grabbing the attainable—but not when the same ball was four feet away. *Distant* space may still be only a flat picture, a neutral zone. Without prior reaching experience, these infants plainly discriminated distance and started their visually guided reaching only to balls they knew they stood a chance of getting.

The First Tools

To describe a baby's growth, the old saying "One thing leads to another" should really read, "One thing leads to an explosion." The perfection of vision and the ability to hold his head up allow appreciation of visual space. The evolution of increasingly efficient reaching also lets the baby appreciate and participate in his three-dimensional world.

You may notice that your baby can grab toys with either hand. This is partly because the baby has mastered the ability to grasp an object even if it touches his hand lightly or his eyes are averted. By the end of the fourth month, he can probably alternate hands to grab the toys or transfer a toy from one hand to the other. He may even wave it exuberantly, then transfer it and repeat the waving—shuttling it back and forth between hands like an amateur juggler. In imitating the behavior of one hand with the other, the baby may be becoming aware that he can do the same thing with each arm and that each hand is distinct from the other. This awareness is very important to his stockpiling of information about space. The baby also begins to see himself act when he repeatedly reaches for and grasps things. He starts to distinguish himself from the outer world.

If you would like another sign of this growth process, try one of Gesell's measures of mental growth, the behavior of a baby before a mirror. According to Gesell "norms," a baby will smile at his image at around twenty weeks of age. Hold your baby up to a mirror and watch him examine the faces there. He will probably attend most to his own image and perhaps smile at it. As his image returns the smile, he may become active and vocalize. He may also look back and forth between your image and you as if the duplication puzzles him. A baby who knows his mother's face cannot understand two of them. Calling softly to your baby as he looks at your confusing double complicates matters even further. His turning back to the real you shows that preference and clear discrimination are possible at four months.

An early attachment to one object—a toy or a stuffed animal—is another index of discrimination, as well as self-development, for the baby's interests are going beyond himself. Most babies do not prefer one toy this early, but some will. After exploring each toy in his crib, your baby may start reaching and playing with one special one, perhaps a set of clacking, plastic disks on a chain. In the months to come, the toy or anything else the baby identifies with himself by wearing or carrying may become a "lovey." "Lovies," or security blankets, as they are commonly called, can be anything from stuffed animals to shoes, a piece of clothing, a diaper, or a blanket which will be played with, cuddled— and dragged around when your baby is nine or ten months old. A "lovey" will be slept with, chewed, hugged, loved, and "talked to." Removing it for brief periods, even for the best of reasons—like washing—may pose real problems. A baby can eventually identify so closely with his "lovey" that a pediatrician can preview each step of an examination with it—put his stethoscope on it, flash his light at it, and thump its "back" to put the baby at ease.

The attachment of babies to such objects, obviously substitutes for mother, helps in the transition to independence from her. If you just think for a moment of how difficult this transition must be, you will realize the value of "security" toys for your baby. They give him another way to cope with the necessary separations from you, as well as the other frustrations of just plain growing up. A highly active baby needs a soft toy for a special reason. Giving up action and play and comforting himself are difficult tasks for him. A friendly, familiar toy bear may just make him easier on himself. Rather than feeling threatened, a mother should be very flattered by her baby's extension of affection elsewhere. Only babies sure of their mother's love will stretch and grow beyond this critical relationship. A baby with the heart to find a "lovey" is showing early resourcefulness and resilience.

Toys Are Also People

Another offshoot of the baby's increased sensory powers is greater interest in toys and people. Toys that he can handle, move around, and change are good right now, as well as later on. Toys are to children what books and records are to many grown-ups. They are mentally stimulating. Toys not only keep a baby from being bored, they help him learn —about space relationships, color, texture, and a world of other things.

For most four-month-olds everything is a game. Watch your baby as he finds he can produce sounds. He will practice

them over and over. At each new one, he may stop in surprise and begin again. His face screws up and his arms and legs become active as his whole body works with the effort. As he becomes more intense, activity may break up his vocalizing for he still cannot carry on both at this pace.

Watch him as he is pulled to stand. He may actually chortle with self-satisfaction and pride. During his bath, he gurgles and laughs aloud, kicks up and down, throws his arms out and splashes water everywhere. He giggles with delight at loud screeching sounds he makes and squeals if his noise-making fetches you from the other room. When one of his sibs gets down in the playpen with him, he can double his playtime up to an hour or more.

He may even have a special game he plays with his family. As early as two months after the baby's birthdate, mother may imitate the baby's cough. At first her cough and smile only attract the baby's attention, but eventually he coughs in return and starts an exchange. The cough, by the way, sounds like a smoker's dry hack. Later the baby initiates the game by coughing and smiling when mother least expects it. The game's value increases as the baby realizes his cough brings his parents rushing when he wants some excitement. While some coughing at four months may be caused by the increased salivation that goes with teething, the baby's "social cough," like an adult's, can be produced at will. Mothers often credit the baby with inventing the game all by himself.

Recognizing authorship is less important than awareness that the coughing game, like most games he or his family will devise for him, is a real learning device. He learns that vocal sounds, like tongue clicks and coughs, are very effective in initiating socializing. He learns that his behavior can effect his environment positively—something very important for a baby to know. Above all, he learns how to imitate oral sounds, an ability essential in language learning.

By the fourth month even the most active baby will devote at least equal time to social contact. A familiar face can interrupt his most vigorous gymnastics. He will look at it, smile to it, and then try a compromise between talk and action. Picking him up prompts eager vocalizing, a real laugh, and looking at your face. Anything that disrupts his play causes displeasure. Since most early conditioning for play is on the back, turning him over onto his tummy may bring a roar of protest, or make him dig his face into the bed, and lie motionless until someone moves him. To condition your

baby to like lying on his tummy, get down on his level and play with him. Gradually, he may begin to play on it, for a while anyway, just as a change of scene.

While most babies increase their responses when parents or sibs are around, some will do just the opposite. Your presence, for example, may actually silence instead of promote vocalizing. An extremely sensitive baby may interrupt his private sessions of cooing, vowel practice, tone play, and careful self-listening to cautiously watch your face and movements. Rest assured that in time he will cope with your appearance and respond to your sounds with his own.

First Visit

The best time to take the baby out with you socially is during his first six months or so. It will not be this easy again for a long time. He is still eminently portable, light, and easy to carry. Soon he will be more aware of his surroundings and the people in it and may not sleep as well in an unfamiliar bed. Until then, not capitalizing on his mobility is a shame. In some ways, this is also the easiest time to take a baby along when you travel. He will sleep happily in any container you make him snug in. In addition, the motion and hum of cars, trains and planes are soothing to most babies. A number of products are available today that make it easier to travel with a baby. Prepackaged formula that needs no refrigeration comes in disposable cans in ready-to-use or concentrated form. Also, there are disposable diapers, diaper liners, and bibs, as well as towels and washcloths saturated with cleansing lotion. Most baby preparations come in light, nonbreakable plastic containers. Unless you are going to out-of-the-way places, you need not stock up and carry a lot of equipment with you. Products like these are available at most drugstores and many grocery stores throughout our country.

Carriage rides, outings to shops, and excursions to houses of relatives and friends, where the baby can be parked in a bedroom, can help dilute sensitivity to strange people, animals, objects, and places and gradually expose and condition him to the world. Sometimes the baby is simply unused to coping with more than his usual two adults.

However, because of the excitement of new stimulation and audiences, he may react rather dramatically after a visit —especially a long one. He may refuse his food, wake periodically throughout the night, and respond to your atten-

tion only to cry himself back to sleep after you have left. His upset can last for several hellish days of crying and whimpering at night and during the day. If hysteria does erupt, a firm, consistent reaction is probably necessary. Your distress is very likely to compound the baby's. A day or so of calculated indifference to his turmoil and bids for attention should help the baby settle back into his normal pattern.

If you do go out and leave the baby home, be sure the relative, friend, or baby sitter you leave him with can be trusted to do things for the baby the way you do. Have her visit first while you take care of him so she has a chance to see the way you hold, handle, play with, and talk to him.

Most four-month-old babies know their mothers, and although about half of them will adjust when a stranger is near them, the other half will rebel. After all, no other person besides you has given so many different and potent kinds of stimulation. If the baby sees you and your friend or sitter at the same time, it is easier for him to establish a connection and to make the transition from friend or sitter to you. (Imagine how panic-stricken and abandoned you would feel if you woke up suddenly in the night to find everybody you loved gone and a stranger standing by your bed.) A little later, in the ninth month, all this changes even more dramatically so you might as well take these precautions and use this stage of your baby's life to get out once in a while.

Motor

Large

Moro reflex begins to vanish.
On back, keeps head in
midposition.

Turns head in all directions,
seated or lying. Holds head steady
and erect for short time.
On tummy, lifts head 90 degrees
from surface, or on straight arms,
or with weight on forearms.
On back, may crane neck forward
to see hands catch feet.

Lies on tummy, legs extended.
May deliberately flex muscles from
waist down, raising hips.
On tummy, may rock like an
airplane, limbs extended and back
arched.
On tummy, rolls from side to side.
May roll from stomach or side
to back.

If pulled to stand, extends legs
and keeps body in same plane
from shoulders to feet.

Sitting

Sits supported ten to fifteen
minutes, head erect and steady,
back firm.

Small

Uses hands more agilely and with
more variety. Mutually fingers
hands. Unskilled mitten grasp,
palm and fingers appose thumb.
May take small objects between
index and second fingers.

Retains doll-size objects.

Swiping still inaccurate.
May look from object to hand,
to object, often misses, but can
grab it. Hands may meet below,
beyond or in front of object.

Language

Active

Cooing becomes pitch
modulated. Sustains it for fifteen to
twenty minutes.
Begins babbling, strings of
syllable-like vocalizing.

Voice quality normalizing; strong,
steady cry.

When talked to, smiles, squeals,
coos.

Vocalizes moods of pleasure up to
thirty minutes—chortles,
squeals, gurgles, giggles, grins,
laughs aloud.

Imitates several tones.

Please do not regard this chart as a rigid timetable. Babies are unpredictable. Some perform an activity earlier or later than the chart indicates.

Growth Chart

Mental

Vision approximates that of adult. Sees in color. Lens of eye adjusts to objects at varying distances.

May increase responsive periods to an hour or more at a time. Sustains interest in details.

Head and eyes turn in coordination and parallel to surface on which he lies or sits; follows dangling or moving object, sound source. Regards ring or rattle immediately.

Activates arms and trunk, looks from hand to nearby object, reaches for, grabs and lets go of it with either hand. Pulls dangling object toward him. Carries object to mouth. Swipes with one arm and open hand but often misses.

Aware of differences in depth and distance. Manipulates table edge slightly. Stares at place from which object drops.

Has memory span of five to seven seconds.

Smiles and vocalizes more to an actual face than to an image. Discriminates faces from patterns, people from things. Discriminates among faces. Knows mother. May resent strangers.

Fingers hands in mutual play. Becomes aware of their distinctness. May smile and vocalize at mirror image. Begins to adjust responses to people. Becomes aware of distinctness of his act from external result, himself from outer world and other objects.

Aware of strange situation. Associates growing number of behaviors. Discriminates; may prefer one toy to others.

May transfer a toy from one hand to the other.

Social

Personal

Vocalizes moods, enjoyment, indecision, and protest. Laughs while socializing; wails if play is disrupted. Shows anticipation, excites, breathes heavily.

Attempts to soothe self. Quieted by music. Clasps fingers and hands in play.

Interested in and may smile at his mirror image. May discriminate mother's image from his. May wait for a feeding.

Interaction

Vocalizes to initiate socializing— coughs or clicks tongue. Responds to and enjoys handling; vocalizes when pulled to sit, not content to lie down.

Shows interest in playthings; may prefer one toy (shows awareness of something outside self). Enjoys play, games, socializing. Doubles playtime if it involves socializing.

Cultural

Interest in feeding decreases due to social interest. Anticipates food on sight or upon hearing preparation. Recognizes bottle and purses mouth for food.

Solids clearly established.

Predictable interval between feeding and bowels.

Splashes in bath, kicks, and lifts head.

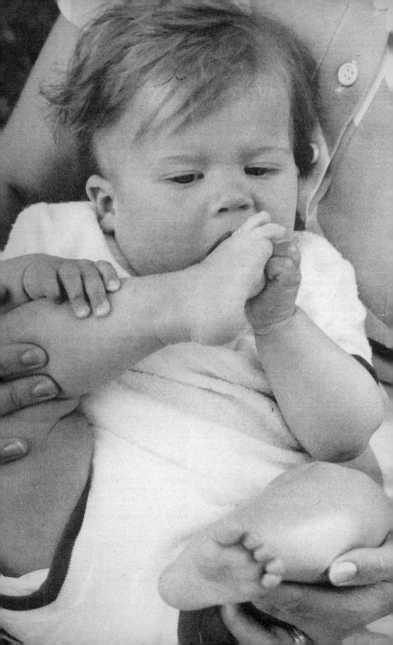

THE FIFTH MONTH
Reaching Out

THE FIFTH MONTH
Reaching Out

Brace yourself. For most babies, the fifth month is the first phase of a fantastic speedup of activity that will leave you breathless by the end of his first year. The quiet of the first four months is over. The baby's attention span, and that means playtime, has stretched to one and one-half or two hours with a little help from you. True, the baby can still do quiet things, particularly when they involve differentiating himself from his world. He can turn now when you call his name from another room or he hears it in a stream of conversation. Mirrors still please him and he will even stop crying to look and smile at himself. This self-interest is very different from an adult's egocentrism. The baby's self-exploration is a healthy first step in extending beyond himself as he grows. His alternate mouthing of fingers or thumbs and toys is a way of comparing himself with objects in the outer world.

Because of his increasing ability to control the muscles in his trunk and lower back, the baby can sit propped in a chair for long periods. His increasing balance and control of his head and his new ability to grasp things while he is seated are very exciting. He is no longer content just to watch things or people that are out of reach. His eyes, fingers, and mouth work together as he learns and he wants things close enough to feel, hold, turn, shake, and taste. You can easily arouse the force behind this inborn integration by accidentally leaving your baby with a toy he cannot reach. He may suddenly howl in frustration as he discovers he cannot examine it fully.

The ability to reach and grasp, generally apparent around the beginning of the fifth month, has had a long, impressive history. In fact, the period from one and one-half to five months is enormously important for early perceptual and physical development. First of all, the baby must be able to see before he can reach. He is born with the first necessary skill: being able to follow a changing or moving light or any small object that contrasts with its background. This visual tracking only happens if the object is on the edge of the baby's visual field. Once he is looking directly at it, the pattern it presents to the baby's eyes determines whether or not he will continue staring. In 1961, Dr. Robert L. Fantz showed that a newborn will fixate on patterns with clearly defined edges and high contrast areas—for example, bright, white stripes on flat black. This peripheral tracking and pattern fixation quickly develop into the central tracking and eye control that will enable your baby to follow moving patterns at which he is looking and to explore his world visually.

Around the middle of the second month of life, the baby's visual activity and growth surge dramatically. He learns to blink at an approaching object. His eyes work together so that they see one object instead of two. The lens of his eye is able to thicken or thin, depending on the distance of an object, allowing him to see objects clearly by the time he is about three and one-half months old. This new eye ability allows the baby to bring his hands into focus, thus linking sight and touch by a double-feedback system. The eyes see the hand and what it feels, the hands feel what the eye sees. The eye control of the hand leads to hand play such as mutual fingering, then one-armed swiping with a closed fist, then jerky open-handed reaching in which the baby's hand often misses its target. Gradually the baby's aim improves as he looks between hand and object and his "direct hits" increase. Then, shortly before five months, the baby can bring his hand rapidly from outside his field of vision to an object he is looking at and grasp it smoothly. As you may have noticed in your baby, the progression of muscle control has been from eyes, head, and arms to hands and from center to the outside edges of vision.

This exciting growth in eye, hand, and body control, as Dr. Jean Piaget says, is the first major thrust of infancy. It means many things: practical concerns such as buying a bounce chair and babyproofing the house; a family "crisis" of making sure everyone gets enough sleep; and inner matters, such as the baby's mental growth and mother's occasional feelings of rejection.

Before your baby becomes really mobile and more searching, take an inventory with your husband of all the household traps the baby might fall into, and babyproof the house. Since he can already clamber out of his infant chair, a bounce chair or swing should be the next step. It should still be at a reclining angle so that even when he arches forward, the chair can support the lower half of his back. It should also be weighted at the bottom so your baby will not topple it. Because he will dream up things you might never think of, you must take precautions. Keep his chair away from heat sources such as the stove, iron, and toaster and get him a strap for his stroller.

Now that the baby can see very clearly, he can visually differentiate his parents. He may squirm, babble, and pump his arms up and down when he finds his father's or your face in a roomful of people. Since he can now tell which people are not his parents, his sensitivity to strangers increases. He may be particularly sensitive to strange women. When a woman "oohs" and "ahs" at him or tries to pick him up during an outing, he may voice his resentment quite clearly. Fear of strange women is often stronger than that toward strange men, probably because a woman arouses all the associations of sight, touch, smell, taste, sound, comfort, learning, and fun that the baby has had more chance to build with you than his father.

The baby's seeing, handling, turning, and reaching for things also help him grow aware that objects are stable and permanent, each with its own autonomy. Up to about five months of age, the baby's world is more or less a series of things that mysteriously disappear and reappear. The baby's reaching for something introduces the idea that things are beyond and apart and, therefore, separate from him. When he handles an object, he senses that its shape remains the same even though its visual appearance changes as he turns it or as it approaches or recedes from him. He also tries to recapture objects if he loses them. For example, he leans over to look for an object he has dropped to the floor instead of simply staring at the place from which it was released. Or he will search outside his field of vision for an object he has been holding. He will play with a teddy bear, leave it for a while, and relocate it without error or hesitation. He will also anticipate a whole object by seeing only a part, and he can and does free his perception by removing minor obstacles, such as a carriage robe, from his face. But he will still give up immediately if a vanished or abandoned toy does not come readily to hand or eye. He still seems to believe that objects are alternately made and unmade. Some months later, he will realize the most amazing thing of all—things will continue to exist and happen even when they are out of hand and sight and beyond his sphere of influence. The day your baby tries to push your hand to make a top spin or a toy train run is the day you will know he realizes that something or someone else besides him makes things go.

Reaching and grabbing also help the baby grow aware that there is a "before" and "after," a cause and effect in an action sequence of his own making. This means he is beginning to keep track of his own actions in the immediate past. In the next couple of months or so, your baby will know enough about his bottle to rotate it should you hand it to him the wrong way. He will demonstrate recognition of familiar objects by outlining actions he habitually makes to them. The baby sees the teddy bear he likes to swing, and opens and closes his hands in an abbreviated version of the swinging movements. This body recognition is the forerunner of mature mental recognition and a first step toward baby's orienting himself to a goal.

The Family's Early Riser

All these faintly sensed but vital understandings are a lot to handle. The baby is on the brink of a great developmental surge and he actively responds to its excitements and frustrations. The average five-month-old rouses himself literally at the peep of dawn to be about this daily business of learning. The baby's four-hour sleep cycles, which crystallized about his third month of life, make him waken about 6:00 P.M. Now, however, instead of lying quietly sucking his fist or looking at his toys, he quickly awakes to practice all his new muscular and social skills. Although he can temporarily amuse himself with rocking spread-eagled on his tummy or turning himself over, he will eventually begin to demand some attention. His crying and calling arouse the household and invite his family away from sleep to share his full day.

No parental maneuver can really impede this inner primal clock. Keeping a baby up later in the evening will not make him tired in the early morning. Feeding him at night does not help. Black shades to keep out the light that moves him are worth a try. Harnessing him to the bed may be an immediate, strong-armed answer for the desperate, but its long-range consequences are not much of a "solution" for anything. Odd as it may seem, harnessing the baby is likely to hurt his physical development less than his emotional growth. More than enough evidence from around the world suggests that physical restraint like tight swaddling only retards motor development by about a month. It is important to reinforce a baby's effort to practice and maneuver. This way you will encourage him to develop mastery over his environment.

Putting the baby farther away from the family is perhaps the kindest solution for all concerned. It not only gives you more sleep, it nudges your baby back to his own resources for a longer time.

For most babies, these antic urges spurt and ebb. But a quieter baby handles his developing awareness more subtly. Grasping and sucking on fingers, toes, and toys intensify as he lies content on his back or brings his feet to his mouth. He mouths and chews every available edge of a toy, savoring each separate fact and flavor of it. Many more active infants are only happy when they are in continuous motion—performing on their own or handled vigorously. Most free on his back, an active baby may kick against his crib mattress or the carpet, and propel himself into a corner where he wedges himself, or he may also twist his body to pull the upper half over and roll onto his belly, then prop himself up on his arms, look about, and roll back again. On his tummy, desperate wriggling with his arms and legs and fierce seesawing may also propel him. At night, a really active baby may wake several times because of the added excitement of this developmental surge. During the semiconscious phase of his sleep cycle, he can wake up fully, and try to comfort himself with activity because it is a characteristic outlet for him. Unfortunately, activity is not the solution to quieting down at nighttime.

Pinning him down with a sheet or blanket or tilting the mattress to prevent his rocking and rolling will only make him fight more furiously whenever he wakes. A late-night feeding and a short play period will release some of his energy more profitably. As little as two weeks later, you may be able to cut out your baby's night life.

Another way to help your baby work off some of his energy and frustration is daytime exercise sessions. You can teach your baby how to roll himself over from back to stomach. You can also show him how to calm himself as he builds to peaks of rolling. Dr. Brazelton suggests that you "flatten the baby on his tummy and bring his thumb to his mouth. Then hold him." The baby may be outraged at first with your intrusion, but eventually he should begin to quiet during the practice sessions and later during the night if he has learned what you mean. This kind of assertive yet loving intervention contrasts sharply with more forceful restraint. Insistent or tactless teaching efforts can assault an infant's sensitivity and cut his desire to learn for himself.

Serious Language Study

You would think that with all this energy devoted to physical development, your baby would have no time for anything else. Not at all. This is the month your baby obviously starts serious "language study." As you may have guessed from your own experience with your baby, expressive language starts not with the first word, but with his first use of cries to attract attention. Scientists agree that at about one month of age, and even earlier according to some mothers, infant cries of discomfort, pain, and hunger can be discriminated by his listener. In the next few months, cooing, squeals of delight, scolding, and grunts of disgust clearly show his reactions to situations. The gesture language of looking and reaching is yet another pipeline of communication between mother and baby. As usual, a baby will approach these efforts in characteristic style. Keep in mind that not all infants are equally interested in speech. The earlier babblers may be the talkers, the ones disposed toward language and that kind of interaction. Some of the "talkers" will screech for the sheer pleasure of experimenting with their sound equipment, while others display a subtle and varied register of tone, quiet trilling, and volume control. Silent babies may be too busy sizing up their world to spend much time "talking" about it. Quiet ones may digest and explore speech and other sounds more privately. An acoustically sensitive baby may, for example, combine listening adventure with producing sounds—his own or mechanical ones. The tinkle of a bell-toy can hold him spellbound. He may even learn to turn it so that it makes different tones. If he prefers to control and produce slight changes in sound himself, the drawn-out variations of a music box may be less absorbing. This combination of extra-sensitive hearing and tone production are basics of good musicianship, so keep an ear out if your baby shows these attributes.

Most babies will communicate with anyone who is available. Your baby will probably watch mouths, jaws, and faces as people make sounds to him, then experiment with his

own vocal and facial movements. His accidental combining
of vowels with the few consonants he knows (*d, b, m* are
usually among the first) sometimes leads to words like *dada,
baba,* and *bye-bye* which thrill the whole family. Since feedback may be one of the most important elements in early
speech learning, a baby's family should always respond to
him. *Dada* repeatedly brings father, and *bye-bye* prompts
delighted squeals from his sister. Even though he cannot
associate sequences of sounds with their word meanings yet,
he learns to imitate himself and to repeat what were originally
trial and error combinations to get the expected response.
A pattern of joyful exchange set, the baby will also try to
imitate the inflections in your voice and move on to more
and more complex language successes.

Besides encouraging this important practice and its companion, a feeling of mastery, this reinforcement has even
more specific teaching functions. The identification of people
and objects is based on the general principle of naming.
Once acquired, it lays the entire foundation of a human
being's ability to symbolize. If you have listened carefully
to your baby, you will quickly realize that at first most of
his sounds are not those of any language, let alone English.
Sometimes the baby will also use sounds like a gutteral *r*
or nasalized "vowels" that are really more appropriate to
German and French. As English-speakers, you and his father
generally respond to the sounds that seem most like those of
English and, of course, your sounds, which are English, are
models for your baby. In response to this selective reinforcement, the baby's non-English sounds very gradually, almost
imperceptibly drop out. Many months later, your toddler will
have a system of real English sounds. Do not expect perfect
English. More than three quarters of your tot's speech sounds
will be clear by the time he is two, but there is an important
difference between understandable English *sounds* and understandable English. The distribution of vowels to consonants
is also very important. Only by about two and one-half will
this distribution approximate that of an adult. What is more,
the sound system of English is only one of three major
aspects of language your youngster is going to learn. The
other two are its vocabulary and grammar.

Social Uses of Early Language

A baby will deliberately use his newly found vocal skills
to intrude upon your attentions to other things so you will

focus them where he thinks they should be—on him. He may start to smile and vocalize to a visiting friend. When this does not stop her chattering, he may twist around and try to divert you. If this fails, you may be stunned and amused to find your baby babbling more and more loudly. To continue your conversation, you may have to remove him from your lap or to another room. Do not be intimidated if the baby suddenly disintegrates into frantic activity or crying. These conversational exchanges are still a great effort for him. Your interaction is as important as your fear of "teaching" him beyond his endurance. Human stimulation of infant sound is vital. Research with infants born to deaf parents indicates that before six months of age, parental inability to hear and imitate an infant's sounds hardly influences their quality. Their cooing and babbling are very much like those of normal babies. But later the lack of response and the differences in his parents' sounds start to influence those of the baby. They lose intonation and grow nasal in quality. Conversely, a hearing loss handicaps a child so much that he can behave autistically—out of touch with his environment. He may have a faraway look in his eyes and withdraw into repetitive, self-stimulating habits to fill the deficit of stimulation from the outside world.

One of the major handicaps of institutionalized toddlers and educationally deprived youngsters is their inability to communicate. Dr. Bettye Caldwell ascribes this to lack of language stimulation. The infant's caretakers have neither the time nor often the interest to talk to him. During the first year of life, there *is* a natural unfolding of language and physical events that the environment can speed or delay, but never reorder. We cannot, for example, teach a baby to utter prepositional phrases before he babbles. The important thing is to talk to your baby.

The fostering of speech begins with mother's encouraging, affectionate sounds and gestures as she feeds, bathes, and makes her baby comfortable. Even at two months, it is more important for a baby to direct his smiling and vocalizing to a responsive face. Speech thus becomes associated in the baby's mind with identification, comfort, and communication. Later, accompanying words with actions, like *all gone* and *up-and-off;* inventing naming games involving baby's nose, toes, feet, hands, and mouth; singing to him and repeating nursery rhymes can all help to make speech interesting and pleasant. A home that provides a palate of occasional sounds —a chiming grandfather clock, a music box, bell-toys, or chirping birds, without a confusing blare of background noise —helps to make an infant aware of different sound qualities.

You need not worry about baby talk, especially at this stage. Use it all you want. Every known language community in the world, admittedly or not, provides this special form of its language to its infant members precisely to teach them to communicate. Your baby's word approximations, a normal and necessary aspect of vocabulary development, need not be paragons of precision. Only the number of words attempted should increase. The baby just needs to hear sounds and human speech, and baby-talk words feature both in plenty.

Unneeded, Unwanted, and Unloved

About the fifth or sixth month, many mothers say they feel left out. As their babies become more competent physically, they see the end of their child's need for mother despite the reality that his need will continue for many years. Overreacting to the baby's relative independence is easy. Two kinds of separations by which mothers express these inner feelings are weaning, if they are breast feeding, and returning to work.

If you are breast feeding your baby, you may rationalize weaning in many ways—all justifiable. He is eating enough solids so that he needs only three feedings anyway. With a bottle, other family members can feed him if you are particularly busy. You will not be as tired when you relinquish this extra physical drain. (Unfortunately, nursing can add to a mother's fatigue.) The baby calls you all day and holds out his arms to be picked up when he sees you. His unanswered appeals make you feel guilty, although you "know" that his frustration when you do not always respond can push him positively toward self-sufficiency. Or the baby himself seems disinterested in nursing.

But do not get so wrapped up in your feelings toward your baby that you forget that other mothers and babies are caught up in the same things you are; that they also are experiencing this vast sequence of events and growth. Actually your baby may be showing the first of three major lags in an infant's interest in breast feeding. According to Dr. Brazelton, "This one is generally associated with the sudden widening, visual interest in his surroundings. The second accompanies the tremendous motor spurt of seven months. The third occurs between nine and twelve months." A few babies never lose interest and probably have to be pushed away. When a baby begins to lose interest after nine months, taking him up on it seems appropriate in our culture. He has had enough nutritional sucking and probably does not really need more.

Many mothers around the world nurse children for several years to give them antibodies against disease, as well as the protein, calcium, and vitamins they would not get otherwise, to protect them as best they can from the incredibly high rates of infant deaths in many developing nations. The natural cycle of conception, pregnancy, birth, and lactation is virtually unbroken until menopause. In our culture, the merits of breast feeding for the baby's health decreases as he matures. As long as the mother nurses, her baby accrues the benefits of immunity to some diseases and allergies. But after the initial start, they are not necessary to his survival. The benefit of nursing for the mother's health may be a different matter. According to recent research at Columbia Presbyterian Medical Center, the incidence of subsequent breast cancer for mothers who have nursed a minimum of six to nine months for each of three children or a minimum of nine months for one or two is virtually zero.

If you really want to, you can wean your baby in a week because your milk will decrease as stimulation drops. But weaning is more traumatic for mothers than many think. Besides the emotional jolt, a shorter, less intense version of post-partum depression may also occur due to hormone changes. Many women unconsciously need to fill their "empty arms" when they wean a baby. A baby's close tie to his father can make weaning even harder. It is childish to feel envious of a baby's closeness to his father when you think how much an infant continues to need his mother.

A slow weaning, on the other hand, gives both you and your infant an opportunity to adjust. If you choose this alternative, pediatricians recommend dropping the noon feeding first, the evening one second, and the early morning one last. Late night and early morning are peaceful times uncluttered with the noises of the day or distractions of other children. Whether you wean now or later, the early morning feeding is usually the hardest to give up, especially if you are used to nursing and cuddling the baby in bed, and then putting him back in his crib so you can grab that extra, precious hour of sleep.

Some babies, perhaps yours included, appear to suck their fingers more after they have been weaned. At this stage, the extra sucking probably reflects tension before a burst of physical growth rather than upset from weaning. Any guilt you might feel because you are not "doing as much for him" really mirrors your own confusion more than his.

Having seen their babies through their difficult first months, many mothers also consider returning to work. They have to weigh the balance between a mother's needs and the infant's need for a consistently dependable mothering figure. Many pediatricians and a number of psychologists, even those who have worked in cultures where mothering by many people seems to be the rule, firmly assert that the baby must have one consistent person to relate to as he evolves his style of responding to the world. Being around many people, including father, older children, grandmother, other relatives, and family friends, who may all give him some care, may make the baby more socially competent and better able to simultaneously handle numerous relationships later on. In fact, collective mothering may reduce some problems of the overly intense family unit, like overattachment to the parent of the opposite sex, hostility toward the same sex parent, competition among children for the parents' attention, or between the parents for the child's. Even so, there should be one primary figure among them all that the baby can count on for help, comfort, learning, and attachment. A baby is less likely to form a strong, close bond with another human being if no one has ever had one with him.

The amount, quality, and consistency of a woman's mothering will influence not only the baby's immediate reactions to his separation, but also his personal, mental, and physical growth. A baby is learning so many fundamentals between three and twelve months of life that he is especially prone to intellectual damage if his environment lacks enough stimulation. On the simplest level, a mother's absence can deprive her baby of the hearing, seeing, and touching stimulation he needs, as well as the appropriate environmental challenges that she makes available to him. Your substitute should involve herself with the baby's mental, social, and physical progress even to the point of getting down on her hands and knees, if necessary, and showing the baby how to back down the stairs when he is learning to get around, instead of disposing of him in a playpen or stuffing him with food.

A baby is also cementing his relationship with his mother during the second half of his first year. He may react immediately to her absence, whether parceled out in nine-to-five packets, or prolonged indefinitely. He may cry a lot, reach out to people, refuse food, forget his latest physical exercises, cling when you return home, and fear strangers even more than usual. Unlike the baby who is separated for a long time from mother, however, the baby whose mother returns to him every day will be able to carry an image of her in his mind and anticipate her return, thanks to his improving memory. When you do find a competent woman to take care of your baby, let him—and your other children, if you have them—get to know her ahead of time.

A beneficial side effect of a mother's working is the greater likelihood that her children will play together and turn to each other more. Unless there is already a serious problem between them, your children will not vie for a sitter's attention and affection the way they might for yours because she will not be as important an intermediary.

If you have decided to work, the only thing worse than feeling guilty is not admitting that you do. Guilt about your imagined neglect of your baby affects him. It can cloud your judgment and break down necessary discipline and schedule. He will need firmness as well as tenderness as much as he did before.

If a young mother needs help in identifying and moderating the results of her complex feelings, her pediatrician can be a great resource. If you do not have a pediatrician who can offer guidance, you should try to find one who can. Remember that there is a time to yield to your needs. You may be more giving of yourself with your children if you are satisfied and practice a total commitment to mothering when you *are* home.

Father: Who Needs Him?

The father's behavior as well is definitely related to his baby's development of attachment. Babies with fathers who helped care for them, played with them often, and were relatively patient about their fussing became attached to them early and intensely. They smiled, vocalized, reached for, and tried hard to make physical contact with their fathers. Dr. Frank A. Pedersen, a research psychologist at the Social and Behavioral Sciences Branch of the National Institute of Child Health and Human Development, considers this attachment very valuable. He speculates that the father enhances his baby's independence by being interesting and desirable enough to draw the baby beyond the mother-infant duo.

Motor

Large

On tummy, lifts head and chest high off mattress.
On back, lifts head and shoulders. Brings feet to mouth and sucks on toes.

Lies on tummy, arms and legs extended.
On tummy, rocks like an airplane, limbs extended and back arched.
Rolls from stomach to back.
On tummy, pushes on hands and draws up knees.

May locomote by rocking, rolling, and twisting; or on back, by kicking against flat surface.
Easily pulled to stand. When supported under arms, stands and moves body up and down, stamps one foot, then the other.

Sitting

Sits supported for long periods (thirty minutes), back firm.

Seated or pulled to sit, holds and balances head steady and erect continuously. Helps in pulling up body, flexes head forward, flexes trunk, draws legs toward tummy.
Seated, can grasp object.

Small

Partial thumb apposition, still precarious. Grasps object with thumb and forefinger, hand partially turned.

Plays with rattle placed in hands.
May hold bottle, one or two hands.

Reaches for ring and grasps; aim good.

Swaps objects from hand to hand.
Grabs or waves object with either hand.

Language

Active

Utters vowel-sounds—ee, ay, ey, ah, ooh, and a few consonant-like sounds (d, b, l, m).

Vocalizes spontaneously to himself, to toys.

May use babble to gain attention.

Watches mouths closely, experiments with own sounds after hearing others.
Tries to imitate inflections.

Passive

Responds to human sounds more definitively; turns head, seems to look for speaker.
Understands name.

Please do not regard this chart as a rigid timetable. Babies are unpredictable. Some perform an activity earlier or later than the chart indicates.

Growth Chart

Mental

Alert up to an hour and one-half to two hours. Looks about in new situations. Turns head deliberately to sound or to follow vanishing object.

Eyes cooperate in grasping and manipulation.
Raises hand in vicinity of an object; alternately glances between hand and object; gradually closes gap and grasps.
Picks up block on contact.
Reaches for object with two hands from sides to middle of his body, sometimes with closed fists. Hands may meet below, beyond, or in front of object.

Wants to touch, hold, turn, shake, mouth, taste objects. Manipulates table edge actively.

Anticipates a whole object by seeing only a part.
Visually searches for fast-moving objects and objects he has looked away from. Leans over to look for fallen object. Removes minor obstacles to vision from face.

Recognizes familiar objects. Remembers his own actions in the immediate past.

Has mental model for human face. Discriminates parents and sibs from others. May resent strangers, particularly women.

Deliberately and systematically imitates sounds and movements.

Tries to maintain through repetition interesting changes he can make in his environment.

Holds one block, regards second. Drops first to take second.

Social

Personal

Shows fear, disgust, anger.

Discriminates self and mother in mirror.
Smiles and vocalizes to mirror image. May bang playfully.

Makes face in imitation.

Interaction

Smiles to human faces and voices.
May distinguish familiar and unfamiliar adults.
Smiles or vocalizes to make social contact.

Shows anticipation, waves and raises arms to be picked up.
Tries to get close to person near crib.
Clings when held.

May learn to tease.
Vocalizes to interrupt others' conversation.
Stops crying when talked to.

Expresses protest—resists adult who tries to take toy.

Frolics when played with.
Plays with rattle, pats bottle or breast.

Cultural

Interest in breast feeding lags.
Takes solids well.
May start on cup.

Wakes promptly at dawn.

THE SIXTH MONTH
Sitting Pretty

THE SIXTH MONTH
Sitting Pretty

The world of the six-month-old has truly become a sitting-up world which he can handle, "talk" with, and play in. Visually alert almost half his waking hours, he can sit for long stretches in a bounce chair and play with toys for at least two hours. In his chair, he can visually follow objects at many different distances and speeds. He can crane over to reach and look at his feet or reconnoiter the surrounding territory. He can bounce over to intriguing objects, reach for anything he sees, and look at anything he manages to grab. This apparent mania to look and grab accurately is critical to your baby's awareness of things in his environment even though it may seem that all your good decorative art will be demolished.

Your baby can probably sit and balance well by himself for approximately half an hour. He can even balance on an adult's shoulders, holding onto his friend's head for support. The gradual appearance of a straight back as he sits and as you gently pull him up to sit reflects a slow downward extension of muscular control. His hands will also tell you how new his sitting skill is. Even after he can sit alone, a baby will use his hands and arms for balance. When your baby manipulates a toy as he sits unsupported, you will know he has become secure in his prowess.

Although he still has to be helped to sit, he can occasionally roll into a near-sitting posture by bending himself in the middle as he rolls. Some very active infants can already get themselves to sit if they get into a crawl position, sit back on their legs, and stick them out in front.

A six-month-old can also arch his back and look upside down at things, twist in all directions, roll, flop, and creep. Dressing him may become a judo contest in which you ply him with a series of toys each of which works only a short time. In preparation for crawling, the first effective way to get around, a baby will inefficiently worm his way across a room by twisting and rolling. You may have to constantly extract yours from under furniture.

A baby this age may also crouch on his hands and knees and hurtle himself forward, only to splatter as he flops with outspread limbs. He may aim a series of flops at a desirable object, which can mysteriously disappear under his body if he overshoots his target. Some babies can even creep with their tummies pressed to the ground, pushing with their feet and steering with outstretched arms. It is unlike crawling, which features bent knees and elbows.

In both flopping and creeping, a baby often goes backward first. Although he may try to move forward, he cannot count on his sense of direction yet. He will go backward more often than forward. Only after quite some time will this reverse.

The early decision in favor of forward instead of backward propulsion must partly depend on a developing awareness that forward is faster. Nature is no help at this point either, because the muscles that enable forward direction are still not as strong as those that push him backward.

Many babies love to stand or be stood up at this age, supported by their parents or holding onto objects. In their infant chairs, they can stand with substantial support. At first, your baby may practice holding on. As he grows competent, he may support himself with only one hand and hold up the other.

A very few six-month-olds will insist on moving from one spot holding onto your hands. Although this generally doesn't happen until about the ninth month, your baby may grunt or fuss at you until you let him go somewhere. With one, then the other stiffened leg, he will swing out like a tiny robot, body rigid and face puckered as he concentrates all energy on his new task. Of course, he's on his way toward real walking.

Dr. Brazelton notes that the remarkable energy flow in an infant's long practice hours "can hardly be reproduced by an adult. Jim Thorpe, the famous four-star athlete, is said to have imitated each move in a baby's active day. He gave out, exhausted, after four hours. The infant continued for eight or more." The infant's relentless practice of his sensory, physical, and mental abilities, in fact, testifies that the need to learn is at least as important as pleasure-seeking in determining behavior during the first two years of life.

Speaking Out

Just as locomotion is a way to get about in physical space, language is a way to get about in the social world. It allows a person to express his wants and influence the people around him. The sequence of motor and language events in your baby's life are so universal that you can pretty much predict where the baby is at in his language learning from what he's practicing physically. Although a six-month-old's vocal efforts may dwindle while he practices physical tasks, verbal expressiveness and continuous babbling are the order of the day. He can grunt or complain when he gets into difficulty, coo or gurgle with quiet pleasure, squeal with excitement, giggle in play, chortle with self-satisfaction, belly laugh with power, growl or fuss with frustration. He can vary the volume, pitch, and rate of his babbling.

Babbling—long strings of vowels loosely connected with consonants—is among the first real signs of language growth. It is so gratifying to a baby that he'll practice his interminable strings with or without benefit of an approving audience. He loves to hear his own voice.

For girls, babbling seems a sign of mental competence. Baby girls who babble to faces and vocalize often in testing situations tend to be more attentive and obtain higher intelligence scores as toddlers and as adults than those who vocalize less. Possibly, scientists speculate, girls are "wired" to verbalize more when an interesting event captures their attention. Perhaps infant vocalization scores better predict

future I.Q. for girls because their overall rate of mental development is more stable. No one really knows yet.

Your baby's babbling repertoire may include "ga-ga-ga" or "ba-ba-ba." When his brother ignores him, he may call something close to his brother's name. Of course, since his parents are the most important people in his world, he is very likely to say *Dada* and call *Mama. Dada,* one of the first infant vocalizations, is linked quickly to diversion and fun. Since you mean business, feeding and relief of difficulty, *Mama* may be voiced at first with overtones of complaint. Even when he's not in trouble, he may call you "for the hell of it." As you rush to avert disaster, you may find him safely on his back, pleased at your appearance. Don't be angry. He is just practicing his skill in naming and calling loved ones. It is important that he try out his power over the world.

Babies who have learned to expect a response from their environment trust it, and are more flexible than those who have called and cried in vain too often. Babies in a nursery with few adults adapt much more slowly to a regular daily feeding schedule and night sleep when they are shifted to one caretaker than babies who have had one-to-one care all along. These babies have learned that they can expect regularity in response to their intitiative. By calling you, the baby has learned to strip down to a very neat signal the behavior that brings your rewarding appearance.

As your baby learns to make sounds, still mostly vowel-like, his appreciation of other sounds will increase. Music may excite him so much that he will babble more, hum, sway, or bounce rhythmically in his chair.

Human speech, especially mother's voice, is a very important part of a baby's sound environment. By this time, it has already acquired significance. Any sound will temporarily stop a baby's babbling as he listens to it. Music stops the baby's vocalizing longest. But voices make the baby pay attention hardest, and only voices make the baby babble more after his initial pause. Babies also babble back most to female voices. The baby is not only differentiating male from female, he is also responding appropriately to his experience. Who, after all, has been his constant language teacher, other than mother?

Recent research at Harvard's Center for Cognitive Studies indicates that talking to a baby is crucial to mental growth. In a study using the familiar peek-a-boo game, a four-month-old baby watched a rubber toy appear and disappear. Its reappearance was sometimes silent, sometimes marked by its own squeak, sometimes by mother's speech. Her voice was the only condition that reliably produced the baby's smile of recognition. Silent reappearance of the object never did. Research also indicates that even a two-month-old is quite able to associate sound with its source, and he can grow very disturbed at any change in production, location, or volume. The localization in space of a sound guides the infant's *visual* attention to the information source. Sound stops and highlights the relatively continuous flow of the visual world. Language plays an important role in skillful development of attention, perhaps *the* critical mental accomplishment of the first year of life.

A Special Style

Since this is the first month that physical activity is really remarkable, differences in style grow more apparent. A baby will select stimulation compatible with his disposition just as he will resist coercion, and each baby will handle coercion differently from his peers. Some babies spend most of their waking hours practicing how to sit, roll over, or creep. Others lie quietly, looking at and listening to things. There is just no prescribed learning order or speed.

Some infants become interested in their hands only after they have mastered large movements like sitting and standing. A few master both areas—small muscles and large movements—simultaneously. Some first learn to control the small muscles of their bodies—signaled by interest in their hands—and then master large movements. They may flop to one side or the other of their chairs and remain immobile when placed on their tummies. Your baby may be limp as you lift him. He may not even try to hold up his head. When you seat him on the floor his legs may poke out determinedly left and right instead of forming a triangular brace for balance. He may slump forward until his chin almost grazes the rug. If you try pulling him to stand, his legs and trunk sag. If you hold him up under the arms, he leans over your hands, sags, or sticks his legs straight out at a 90-degree angle to his trunk. This movement, which requires just as much energy as standing, may cue you to something that your baby is trying to tell you. He simply will not be pushed to perform until he's ready to do things himself despite what the neighbors say or what *their* children are doing. You might take the tip.

Keeping your cool about your baby's more sedate motor development may be difficult, especially because of comparisons to other babies' feats. There is no reason to be alarmed or to push him. Although a complete lack of opportunity to practice things like creeping or standing may slow development, the maturing of your baby's muscles is the main antecedent of each physical ability. Bear in mind that there is no requirement that a baby sit, creep, or stand at six months. In fact, most American babies sit and creep at seven months, and stand at nine or ten. Infants who respond physically to light stroking of their skin are less likely to exert muscular effort than infants who respond only to more vigorous touching. Quiet babies enjoy being tucked into bed and being dressed, even during the months of intense motor learning, and may prefer cuddly toys. Quiet infants, it has been suggested, gradually evolve greater attention spans. In school they are more able to concentrate their energies on learning.

Quieter babies also tend to be plumper than active, wiry ones, independent of food intake. According to a fascinating study at Harvard's Department of Pediatrics, thin babies moved more and ate more than average while the extremely fat ones moved and ate less. Fat babies remained fat despite unusually low calorie intake. The researchers found that unusually heavy and unusually thin babies have a smaller and larger number of active cells and, therefore, lower and higher basic metabolism than average. Basic metabolism, which is inborn, is a cause rather than a result of unusual fat proportions. The average, healthy, well-fed baby, it seems, tends to adjust his food intake to his expenditure on activity. Activity was also associated with parental characteristics. Active infants were children of sensitive, nervous, or restless mothers. The less active babies had either more secure and placid mothers or relatively insecure and passive mothers. The children of the placid parents were more likely to increase their activity with age than those of the passive mothers, who presented less stimulating environments.

The mother of an active baby should try not to worry that he sleeps less than most babies his age, or that very little food manages to get into him, or that he is not gaining enough weight. Intelligent, active, curious children, according to several studies, tend to sleep less than average. Your baby's body is geared differently than most and may be more efficient in using food and rest.

Remember, too, that during the first year, energy expended on activity peaks at six months. Your baby needs only a very few calories for growth of new tissues or weight gain. In fact, growth per se uses less than 15 percent of the total calories the baby consumes. The balance is used for daily activity.

Also, a baby simply stops gaining weight from time to time. In one study, infants who gained weight more gradually over a fifty-day period developed motor skills more quickly than infants showing rapid weight gain. Conversely, changes in a baby's body proportions and fat mass require more adjustment in the development of motor skills. In fact, physical, mental, or emotional growth proceeds in spurts, lulls, or regressions. Sometimes a baby economizes in some areas to grow or recover in others. A sick baby lacks energy for complex emotional adjustments or new mental accomplishments.

A mother of a big baby—sixteen pounds and above is heavy at this age—may establish an undesirable cycle. The baby's weight can "immobilize" him. As the baby becomes frustrated with his difficulty in moving, he may want to eat more or mother may feed him more to keep him quiet. This is the worst thing to do, for it will establish an association between eating and relief of discomfort. It also produces excess fat cells that will become a permanent part of the body. Research indicates that an adult who has been significantly overweight since childhood can keep trim only by incessant self-denial. The extragenerous supply of greedy fat cells seems to trigger metabolic changes so that a once-fat man must restrict himself to far fewer calories to maintain a comfortable weight than a man of the same size who has never been fat.

Instead of feeding your baby more, try to encourage activity by playing vigorously with him. Peek-a-boo, for example, may make him bounce and "reach" with excitement. As the baby becomes more active, the fat will be used and absorbed into firmer flesh. Or let the baby find his own way to break the cycle. Keep in mind that the impact of activity on weight is at its height between four and six months. In other words, your baby's inactivity will probably be more responsible for excess weight now. Your baby's food intake, which you can pretty much control, will affect his weight more later on. Your control of his food intake plus promotion of physical activity should do the trick.

Declaration of Independence

If you are still nursing your baby, his new teeth may mean some adjustment for both of you. Of course, it is accidental, but being bitten in such a sensitive place is painful and annoying. An honest reaction—startling or pushing the baby away, or providing a substitute biting object (even a finger) —will help the baby learn that his behavior is unacceptable to you as much as you love him.

Bottle feeding poses its own dilemmas. If your baby is particularly precocious, he may insist on manipulating his own bottle. Let him try it, but do continue to hold him even if he does not seem to want it at first. The most grown-up kind of baby will eventually show his appreciation of the warmth and stimulation of body contact and human exchange. A highly geared baby especially needs this to soothe him to a state where he can absorb the warmth and gratification of feeding times. His energy and drive can push him to a kind of fierce "busyness" that lets in very few cues from his environment.

A six-month-old may relish being started on drinking from a cup. Initially without finesse, a baby's first ventures will probably feature more chokes than swallows. But even breathing liquid up their noses will not daunt some. An infant can become so attached to his cup that he squeals or claps his hands as he sees it coming and cries if he loses it.

Even though a precocious six-month-old can probably master drinking from a cup, he should have the chance to return to his bottle whenever he seems to need it. Such regressions to more "infantile" states are necessary in the hectic pell-mell growth of the first year. Solids are something else. By this stage, your baby may also show definite likes and dislikes. Most babies, for example, refuse spinach, but adore fruits. Many dislike the taste of plain meat. If yours does, you can mix the meat with a vegetable. Most babies can handle it this way. Meat is just too valuable to omit. Its iron and protein are increasingly important as your infant grows and becomes more active.

Mealtimes, you will find, are also a lot messier. The baby is more distractible and active. Feeding him in his bounce chair is worth a try. The tray holds his spoon and cup. Your six-month-old is sloppy and, believe it or not, a rain slicker may be very useful garb for his feedings. A baby can and will refuse to swallow a bite just to tease his mother, grab the spoon from her hand, sling food around the room, blow bubbles with the carrots, and spray the wall with blown-out spinach.

One reason for chaotic feedings is your baby's increased dexterity. He is ready and willing to use his hands. Like most early learning, the baby's first attempts to secure things, edible and otherwise, are terribly rigid. Even a baby's attentiveness at this time is limited by a kind of inflexibility. Researchers at Harvard's Center for Cognitive Studies found that babies around five months of age could not accommodate presentations of alternating objects that appeared less than six seconds apart. They showed a kind of overload reaction, looked puzzled, averted their heads, cried, and sometimes laughed.

To reach, a six-month-old concentrates totally on the task at hand and opens his eyes and hands *wide*. His fingers are stiffly and fully extended, and his trunk and head must be more or less aligned. The reach itself may be with both arms. It looks more like a locked pounce than a smooth act. By the end of the year, though, he will be quite dexterous.

Because of the beginning control of his small muscles, a baby this age may be interested in manipulating bits of food on his tray, closing his palm around them and taking them to his face. At this point he may try to smear the mangled residue into his mouth. Some babies are less awkward than this. A dexterous six-month-old may postpone and savor the coming pleasure of a teething biscuit for many minutes, depending on his style, then bring it to his lips, and lick it all over before chewing on it. Once finished, he may lick his fingers delicately. Giving the baby teething biscuits or little pieces of toast or banana to handle while you feed him his solids will keep him happy and occupied and will encourage his important practice of manipulation.

Games Babies Play

Mealtimes are also the arena for games. A six-month-old loves to clown and make faces. Since meals are key socializing events, a six-month-old is very likely to try out his glad bag of facial tricks with a favorite brother or sister. Since he's not too versatile, the game will inevitably deteriorate into blowing bubbles with his milk and spitting food bits. If you can occasionally tolerate the mess, your baby will learn more than you can calculate. The games babies play help them learn the essentials of getting about in this world.

The tot who stretches his arm to his head level when his father asks "How big are you?" is approaching the vast field of spatial relationships. The eight-month-old who plumps a block into a jar is delving into the notions of container and contained, empty and full, in and out. The ten-month-old who cruises to the stove and pokes it tentatively is ready to learn about heat and cold. The six-month-old whose favorite toy is a piece of paper that he can touch, look at, turn, rattle, crackle, change its shape by bending or rolling, and finally take to his mouth and savor, is experimenting with the properties of objects.

Peek-a-boo, a game that appears about the beginning of the fifth month, is in the same class. Its first version involves the parent hiding his face with his hands, then removing them, much to the baby's delight. The baby soon learns to cover his own face. The game is so instinctive that a healthy infant may draw other relatives into the fun. Sibs play the game more vigorously, leap from behind chairs, roar and yell. The baby is enchanted with either variant and even stops crying to play them. Within weeks of its appearance, the baby himself will invent variations. He draws a diaper over his face, chuckles, and kicks his feet playfully after calling his parents. They ask, "Where is baby?" He squeals with delight and keeps the diaper on. If they remain quiet too long, the baby may vocalize and kick again, then remove the diaper from a startled little face to smile, reassured by their presence. Peek-a-boo may be a first token of humor. Baby has played a trick on someone, and has clearly decided beforehand that he in fact intended to play one.

The game also means the baby has a memory of someone he loves, and her or his image is fixed enough in his mind and secure enough in his feelings for him to try a short separation under his control. It also means that he has a sense of mother's permanence, as well as that of objects, and even anticipates the joy of recalling her.

A bit later, the baby will assay separations in other ways. The come-and-get-me game requires a pursuing parent and a scrambling baby. The game should not be curtailed too quickly lest you end up with a furious infant. Several runs before the abduction of the infant to a meal or diaper change will promote a more resigned capitulation. At about the same age, a baby may begin to look over the edge of his chair at objects that he has dropped to the floor. This is the pick-up-the-things-I-drop game. He will vary this during feeding times by dropping his spoon and cup overboard as he avoids the spoon you proffer. When all dropable items are gone, he will probably cry for mother or sibs to retrieve them.

Like peek-a-boo, this game demonstrates that the baby is beginning to have a concept of himself. He is separate from other people and from objects and can influence them through actions *he* has selected. In a more general sense, his initiation of the game relates to a growing capacity to formulate a goal and take the necessary actions to attain it. Intent matched with a plan is nothing short of intelligent behavior.

Of course, brothers and sisters can expand this repertoire endlessly. Together they can romp around the house. One likely game, of course, is mother, daddy and baby; he is stood, bedded, fed, and diapered like a ragdoll. He will play for up to two hours with this kind of game.

Despite the risks of accidentally being steped on or spilled from a chair, this play is very valuable. As your baby co-operates with his sibs, he develops mentally and socially. He has opportunities to touch, watch, imitate, and listen that he would otherwise never have. He learns he must sometimes "play" a role to hold someone's attention. A brother or sister for the baby is an advantage to you, too. He may violently refuse your feeding but sit quietly for a bowl of cereal or even an entire meal from his sister. On a particularly bad day, you have one more resource on which to rely.

Play with brothers or sisters is so rewarding that a baby will gladly overcome pain, fear or reprimands to keep them near. A baby is a resilient little creature, and almost nothing a brother or sister can do will frighten him. Sibs will distract your baby from his growing pains, fill in your temporary absences, and actually assist in your caring for him. They can stimulate a quiet baby or slow a hyperactive one with pastimes such as "reading" that he would otherwise not tolerate except for his love of them. Because of them, an inner-directed baby will grow interested in something besides his own activity. Play with toys and things that require him to utilize his hands, and sharing play might otherwise be longer and harder in coming. Hopefully, you will agree that this play means so much to your baby and other children in learning to build relationships and growing to love each other that you will carefully monitor, interfere when necessary, but not stop it because of some relatively minor risks.

Motor

Large

Turns head freely.

On tummy, lifts and extends legs high.
Turns, twists in all directions.
Rolls from back to stomach.
May get up on hands and knees in crouch, hurtle forward or backward by flinging limbs out.
Creeps—propels self on tummy with legs, steers with arms, goes backward or forward.

Stands with substantial support.

Sitting

Sits with slight support; balances well. Can lean forward or to side.
Sits in chair, grasps dangling object. Bounces.

Sits alone momentarily. May sit unsupported up to one-half hour. May need to slump forward on hands to balance.

May bend self to near sitting position on side while rolling from back.

Small

Holds bottle.
Rotates wrist. Turns, manipulates objects.

Reaches with one arm.

Language

Active

Vowels begin to be interspersed with more consonants (f, v, th, s, sh, z, sz, m, n, commonly).
Varies volume, pitch, rate of utterance.

All vocalizations still differ from mature language, but more control of sounds.

Babbles and becomes active during exciting sounds.
Babbles back most to female voices.

Vocalizes pleasure and displeasure; grunts, growls or complains; coos, gurgles with pleasure, squeals with excitement, giggles, belly laughs.

Passive

Reacts to differences in intonations and reflections.

Please do not regard this chart as a rigid timetable. Babies are unpredictable. Some perform an activity earlier or later than the chart indicates.

Growth Chart

Mental

Turns, twists in all directions. Coos or hums or stops crying on hearing music. Reacts to changes in volume.

Alert two hours at a stretch. Visually alert close to 50 percent of daylight hours.

Reaches persistently for anything he sees quickly and without jerks. Usually looks at anything he reaches for, but may close eyes. Picks up block deftly and directly.

Likes to look at objects upside down and to create changes in perspective.

Inspects objects at length. Lifts cup by handle. Pulls paper away. Shows interest in containers. Lifts inverted containers.

Reaches to grab and secure dropped object.

Attends to another's scribbling.

Senses the relationship between hands and objects they manipulate.

Transfers object from one hand to the other. Holds one block, reaches for a second. Regards third block immediately.

Social

Personal

Smiles at mirror image. Differentiates self from mirror image.

Alternates hand with object in mouth; alternates hands to hold objects—aware of separate parts of self, self versus world. Tries to imitate facial expression. Turns when he hears his name.

Interaction

Disturbed by strangers. Distinguishes adults from children. Smiles at, reaches out to pat strange children. Calls parents for help.

On back, grasps foot in play. Prefers play with people, especially cooperative games—peek-a-boo, come and get me, go and fetch.

Cultural

Begins to show interest in finger feeding self. Develops strong taste preferences. May want to manipulate own bottle. May start manipulating cup.

Sleeps through night. Sleeps about half of twenty-four-hour period.

THE SEVENTH MONTH
Perpetual Motion

THE
SEVENTH
MONTH
Perpetual Motion

During the second half of this first year of life, your baby's overall body proportions will change rapidly, and he will move from relative immobility to the basic skills that will enable him to get about in his world. For most babies, the seventh month is one big gush of motor development. While your baby has been sitting supported for several months, he can sit all by himself now for many minutes and can be carried comfortably on your hip. The use of his arms and hands, at last free from supporting him, give him a new lease on life, and the greater agility of his trunk lets him begin to wheel around and lean over to pick up objects, which he deliberately drops just to practice his new picking-up skill. He can turn himself over halfway from his stomach and push with his arms on one side to a sitting position. Some will try one side, drop back to the ground and try the other, as if delighting in full exploration of each before settling on one.

The baby's creeping improves visibly and he can count on going forward all of the time. He may start to practice some variations on this theme. Above all, he is beginning to experiment with standing. In the next few months, he will convert his world from a sitting-down to a standing-up one. Of course, the baby's budding ability to get about and his growing activity have far-reaching implications for him and for his family.

Many babies begin to practice crawling this month, the first really effective way to get about. Crawling is a difficult art, according to Dr. Myrtle McGraw, a developmental psychologist at Briarcliff College, who has studied infant physical development for almost forty years. She writes that "nowhere is the struggle between higher and lower brain centers for the control of behavior more clear than in the development of crawling." The higher brain, or cortex, does not take over the movement of all muscle groups in this activity at the same time. It begins with the shoulders and arms and eventually gets to the legs. So for a while at the beginning of cortex functioning, your baby will pull and tug with his arms trying to move himself forward while the legs hang behind like a dead weight. Or he may push up on his hands, straighten his arms and twist from one side to the other. Eventually he might flex his legs and hop on his knees. Some babies will get up on palms and knees, rock back and forth or hurtle forward before really shoving off properly.

Eventually your baby may push up on his legs and "practice" this new accomplishment for hours on end.

For a couple of weeks or so, he may simply teeter on four small stilts. Then he may apply information about locomotion that he gained from creeping and gingerly inch a stiffened leg out and move a little. The first participation of the legs is only half-hearted. One leg goes this way, and one that. An arm swings out twice before a leg can be persuaded to move; and sometimes the baby loses his usual control of shoulders and arms and falls flat on his face. A few more tries and he learns that a hitch with a foot can be followed by a hitch with one arm. The two supports balance better, and he begins to get the leg and arm on one side to work with each other. He plops on his nose many times more before he realizes that he also has to fetch the opposite leg and arm. Ultimately, the body and four limbs begin to work together as a precision team. Dr. Brazelton suggests that there may be inborn corrections between motor acts that feel "right" when made by chance and integrated. These connections send a rewarding signal to the baby's brain, which allows the baby to identify and preempt that piece of experimentation for the next try.

Dr. McGraw was among the first to detail this relentless practice of a motor task until it is thoroughly mastered. Just as the baby practices his ground locomotion for hours at a stretch, so he practices standing. One day you may be lucky enough to witness your baby's first efforts. His playpen is often the easiest place to start. It offers lots of easy handgrips. Or he may maneuver over to a large piece of furniture, like the couch or a buffet, gather his knees under him, pull with his arms and push with his legs. Finally, he has gotten *himself* to stand.

Variations on a Theme

No infant, however, need subscribe to such rituals. Babies differ in the order and speed with which they learn motor skills. A small apartment, unlike a large house, may reduce a baby's incentive to keep up with his mother because he can see and hear her from any room. Some babies will stand between creeping and crawling. This curious interlocking of developmental steps is not uncommon. Some babies become frightened by their sudden ability to stand. As if struck by the need for more ground practice, they plump themselves down again to drill an alternative pattern on hands and knees. After they absorb it, they stand again several weeks later, reassured enough to attack the important step of upright locomotion. Because of this kind of unevenness in growth— the lags and lulls that every baby experiences—you should know when not to drive your baby in a given direction, as well as when to stimulate and encourage the expansion of some performance.

For a very active baby, sitting alone may be old hat at this point, and creeping, passé. On the other hand, a quiet baby may just be learning to inch along by seven months and won't even begin to crawl until the tenth. While creeping usually precedes crawling by several months, your baby's crawling may follow in a month's time. An active baby may navigate by half rolling, half pushing at five months; move with speed at six months; and crawl this month, as against the "average" baby who creeps at six months and crawls efficiently at eight.

Babies also differ in the type of locomotive skills they favor. Dr. McGraw writes of the many fascinating styles with which babies first learn to get about, styles which often seem to reflect the baby's character. One style, a sitting position in which the baby uses one arm for pulling and one leg for pushing, frees a baby's eyes and ears for every nuance in the environment. This sitting posture may be associated with a baby who is extra-sensitive to sights and sounds. It also leaves him in a better position to retrieve toys and to continue playing with them once he arrives at his destination.

An active infant may already be adding other forms of locomotion, ground and upright, to his inventory. He sits and bounces across the floor on his buttocks, a method that replaces creeping for some babies.

A very active baby may also be able to move about standing up, by lunging and grabbing one piece of furniture after another. Although his balance is shaky and he may fall forward repeatedly, his bravado will probably remain unscathed as he gradually refines his judgments.

A quiet baby may quite legitimately be doing very different things. During this month his activity may spurt. He is much more cooperative in sitting when a parent helps him, and he can sit alone by hunching forward and supporting himself on both arms. If your baby is doing this about now, don't leave him this way too long or he will tire the sparse musculature of his lower back. In his own leisurely manner, he will also begin to move. On his back he can mosey along by hoisting his buttocks and pushing with his feet. Since this works him toward new places, he gains incentive to move, not because he enjoys movement in itself as some babies do, but because it brings a change of scene and new visual delights. If he is intrigued with sound as well as sight, he will appreciate the splatting noise of his buttocks as he flops along. He, too, practices for long hours in his own fashion.

To encourage a quiet baby to locomote on his stomach, place a favorite toy just out of reach. As soon as he realizes you won't get it for him, he may hump grudgingly toward it. Selective doses of frustration often give an important and sometimes necessary push toward learning. Make sure the toy itself is attractive. If your baby is relatively indifferent toward motor performance, the strategy may otherwise fail.

This same baby may be quite precocious in the use of his hands. He can use this as an outlet as much as another baby uses large motor achievements. In comparison to a baby who is precocious in both large and small muscular achievement, your baby may be very conservative in sitting, moving, and standing but still excel in manipulative skill. He may amuse himself on his stomach for thirty minutes, fingering a string of small beads of different shapes and textures. He loves to play with a cluster of keys, handling, rattling and mouthing each. He can reach, poke at, and pick up even a minute puff of dust in a thumb and forefinger.

If your baby can sit unsupported on the floor, pick up a cup with one hand, and carry it to his mouth using both hands, then he is precocious indeed. Usually, a seven-month-old can only handle much larger objects. He is not nearly as sophisticated about shape, texture, or his own grasping style.

Now that his thumb fully apposes his fingers, he can grasp blocks or toys comfortably. Joyously he bangs together toys held in each hand or hits one, then the other against the floor or wall, much like his mirrored, alternating arm and leg activity as a newborn. At this stage, play in front of a mirror helps your baby sort the merits of one side against the other —a part of finding out about his world. Although some babies start to prefer the right to left side of their body as early as three or four months, most infants use both hands equally all through the first year. Holding a block in each hand simultaneously previews another new and exciting accomplishment, the use of both hands instead of only one or the other.

Experimentation with his hands is so exciting that a seven-month-old usually appears with something in one or the other. He creeps around a room dangling a toy, and sometimes keeps both hands occupied. Even standing, he hangs onto a support with one hand while manipulating a toy with the other.

Exploring the World

With his increased dexterity, mobility and curiosity, your baby will begin to explore everything as he pulls himself around the house. That is one reason babyproofing your house is so important. Anything to do with electricity should be protected *and* designated as a definite No. Plastic covers should fill up electrical outlets. If the baby's finger is wet or if he pokes his tongue into an outlet, he can burn himself badly. And an electric burn does not heal without scarring. You must also stay close to the baby now on his home-world tours, even though an enjoyable companion will only spur him on to further adventures.

As part of exploring and comparing himself to his world and the people in it, the baby may poke at your ears, nose, mouth, and eyes, as well as his own, and even compare the feel of your features with his. If you suck his exploring finger, he may try sucking it again himself, then offer it for a resampling.

As your baby investigates, he may poke at every part of his body. He has already discovered his ears, nose and mouth and now as he begins to sit and bend forward, he can also see the lower part of his body. But his only real opportunity to find out about his genitals is when he is undiapered. A baby boy may play with and pull his penis until he has an erection. A girl may poke at her vagina.

The pleasure generated when an infant first finds his genitals clearly indicates their greater sensitivity in comparison to other body parts. American practice intensifies the baby's curiosity and pleasure and heightens sensitivity. Our puritan heritage makes us uncomfortable with our bodies and we keep this area hidden and out of reach. Diapers protect the genitals so well that the skin is conditioned to stimulation only with elimination. Other body parts are more exposed to air, temperature changes, pressure, and touch. Then, too, when a baby starts investigating, somebody grabs the deviant hand, distracts him, or covers the area. Reaction varies from embarrassment and moral indignation to real concern, offense, and shock, particularly among adults of the older generation. So the baby may grow especially fascinated with this novel and provoking-to-mother region. Sometimes we justify our behavior by insisting that unless we curtail normal handling the child will damage himself. Any competent physician can assure you that this is not so. The baby's discovery and exploration of his genitals is normal and important now and at all ages, and most babies go through it. Institutional babies are often "stuck" in it because they have nothing more pleasurable or interesting to do. But an infant with emotionally healthy parents and a stimulating environment almost never is.

The baby also goes through some emotional adjustments to his improved mobility. He is often more interested in being included in social interaction, more tense, and more dependent on mother. In his sitting-up world, the baby was willing to sit and watch, smile when his sibs smiled, and gurgle when they laughed. But now he needs to be an active participant. When his "recognize-me-please" need is unanswered, he either creeps into the middle of whatever they are doing or creeps to find you.

The tension before big developmental steps, like sitting and moving about, may show itself in irritability or chewing fingers and thumbs. Some babies actually look vacant and roll or bang their heads so much that their hair wears away until their tension is released in real action. Then these disturbing behaviors taper off except when the baby is tired or hungry, when he suddenly reverts to them. When life is again consistently gratifying, they will disappear as your baby, fancy free, whips through the house—his territory at last.

The baby's new freedom, because of his improved locomoting skill, also exposes him suddenly to increased stimulation from all angles before he has had the chance to adapt to it. His unreadiness, plus the sometimes frightening information he gets in his broadened sphere, make him more dependent and more fearful of separations from you. Heightening this fearfulness is his affection for you. He wants food, attention, stimulation, and approval from you even when others are available to offer them to him. He keeps close to you with a more or less primitive mental map in which you move more or less predictably. He is also more aware of your ability to move (and that means away from him) because he knows through his own experience what moving is all about.

As he performs the motor arts of standing and crawling himself, he becomes aware of their dimensions. As he stands tottering for the first time and has to be helped down, self-conscious and frightened, he becomes aware of the dangers of falling and his own inability to modify his position. Once thoroughly delighted in being pulled to stand by a loving sister, he may now steadfastly refuse to be stood up by anyone but his parents, correctly aware that their competence and judgment are greater than hers, or his. His frightening awareness that he and you can get away from each other precedes real mastery in getting away, and creates some indecision about improving this terrifying skill. The truth is that

you are still much better at getting away from the baby than he is at keeping up with you.

Besides that, he is still very inept and new at his explorations and play, which are admittedly great fun. Perhaps he senses he has little discrimination about the dangers he is dimly aware of and desperately needs your help to retrieve him from the difficulties he is surely going to work himself into. As long as he sees you, he can play contentedly. You may notice that when you leave a room, he cries and tries to follow, and he no longer likes staying in his playpen while you work in another room. Although you may need to keep him in his pen, at least try to help his new dependence. When you leave, turn to tell him you'll return, and call to him periodically from the distance. The vocal contact will be some comfort, and he'll probably call you to check on your location every once in a while. Although sometimes content with this exchange, he may aim himself in your direction, facing the door you might enter or the direction of your voice, or work himself into a frenzy just to get you back so he can cling a little. Don't worry. His drive for independence, plus your reassurance and consistent presence, will press him through his temporary impasse. Attachment to a person or belief is usually most intense just after it is realized, so the baby is most vulnerable now to any brand of separation from you. Remember, too, that only babies who have good relationships with their mothers are uncomfortable with separations. Babies whose mothers make little difference one way or the other react less because they have learned to cope alone and too soon.

Undercover Work

Although the baby again seems to be devoting all his energy to developing his physical skills, he is also working on his mental abilities. His associations are becoming more and more keen. When he hears the front door open and close at night, he sings out to greet his father. Most of it is sheer babble, but somewhere in that stream is something like "dada." He knows that sounds of the refrigerator door mean food, and grunts in anticipation of his own feeding. As his sister imitates him by sucking her own fingers, his laughter demonstrates he already visually associates her act with his. In "reading" with a brother who "meows" for the cats and "bow-wows" for the dogs in a picture book, he crows—

without prompting—at a picture of a baby as if he recognizes it and associates the baby with himself and his own sounds. He has also learned behavior immediately appropriate to his "reading." He discerns that his brother makes a sound for a picture, and does the same thing—correctly. Older women seem fine at first because he connects them with grandmother, but as soon as he takes a good look and hears the voice (corroborating evidence) he bristles with fear and disappointment. He is also becoming aware of size differences and able to sort them. Give your baby blocks of different sizes to play with and watch what he does. If he holds them out in front of him, looks from one to the other, and places them in front of him, then he is really comparing them. As if to digest their size difference, he picks them up again with different hands, mouths each and puts them down again—in reverse order. Such comparing can occur as early as six months, but is more usual now.

He is developing a sense of humor, which often starts with humorous, playful associations with a game or in response to a surprise situation with an adult or child. For example, if you join in your baby's singing to himself, he may stop, smile, and resume humming. He may giggle and even bounce in time with you. Sometimes a segment of the original fun situation may trigger rememberance of all of it and elicit his first response. Dr. Brazelton describes such a situation. You drop something and say "damn," and the baby laughs at the suddenness of the word and at your awkward posture as you pick it up. The association is made. You pull a laugh with a swear word every time as the baby identifies the words, sounds, and emotional overtones. Your baby, incidentally, also reinforces you. A repeated response—the baby's laughter—shows not only a general ability to remember but also the ability to remember segments representative of whole situations. This ability is precocious at seven months but quite possible.

Bits and Pieces

As part of his increased dexterity, many a seven or eight-month-old will begin to pick up bits of food with his thumb and first two fingers at mealtimes. Since he is still awkward, his self-feeding will be messy. If food drops into his closed fist, he will have to work arduously to extract it. His method of getting food into his mouth is to smear it in with his palm.

When finished with what is often a long and laborious process, the baby may mash his leavings into the feeding tray or sweep them onto the floor in a grand gesture of satiety.

Despite his clumsiness, the baby should be encouraged in his desire to feed himself. Letting him participate in simple ways, like supplying finger bits or a spoon and cup for each hand is much easier for you and more informative for your baby. "Many mothers," Brazelton points out, "feel so compulsive about getting food into their babies that they miss the obvious value of the baby's exploratory behavior with it." First, the baby will learn to feed himself. He will also learn more about his environment. Looking at, handling, tasting, and smelling food is part of the same exploring that begins earlier with inedibles. A simple indication of this learning would be the baby's reluctance to finger slippery foods, such as bananas, in contrast to his crumbling cookies and breads beyond recognition. These sensuous experiences with food enhance the entire feeding exchange for your baby. If he is allowed to enjoy his food and permitted to develop his own eating habits, he also learns that the world is not a restrictive, forbidding place where assertion of his own feelings and wants only bring trouble.

In countless passive and not-so-passive ways, a baby can fight a mother who ignores his desire to participate in his own feeding. If the baby can't amuse himself, he may prolong the meal interminably. He may start to tease you by throwing bits of food around, spitting, sputtering, or delicately oozing out food after slowly and scientifically inspecting and turning it in his mouth. He may laugh joyously at his own antics, mouth full, of course. Or, he may fling his head, clench his mouth, or grab for the spoon he wants to manipulate. Chewing and swallowing unwieldy lumps that he feeds himself and refusal of your smaller, more manageable ones signal the greater incentive of independent action.

Many foods can be gummed up in the baby's mouth or swallowed whole if they are diced into small pieces. These should be fed to him in small quantities at a time so he won't stuff himself and choke. Brazelton suggests that a seven-month-old can just begin to manage foods such as the following:

    bits of dry cereal
    bits of soft toast
    French toast
    diced cooked carrot or potato
    peas with skins broken
    scrambled egg
    bits of soft cheese
    bits of soft ground meat
    diced sandwiches with baby beef,
        liverwurst or a spread

"As he learns to gum or chew up the first bits, give him more," Brazelton continues, "two at a time." The deliberation in exploratory use of his hands and fingers will give you time to feed him, or busy yourself around the kitchen.

It is still too early for spoon and fork. Such dexterity comes at about sixteen months. By the time he can stand and walk, a baby can feed himself entirely with finger foods, manipulate bits amazingly well, and drink from his cup with help. Right now, the baby can handle a cup awkwardly. In the first week or so of cup use, a seven-month-old has no appreciation of how to keep the rim of his cup at an angle compatible with the horizontal level of the milk, juice, or water inside. In respect for his rigid handling, try filling the cup only slightly. At fourteen months, the baby will be able to match the cup to water level with four or five corrective movements of the hands, wrists, and elbows as he lifts it to his mouth. By twenty-seven months, these distinct corrections are all gone, and the hand-wrist-arm system fluidly and smoothly maintains the levels of rim and liquid on the way to the mouth.

Feeding Problems

A mother who pressures her baby to eat can cause real feeding problems. Teasing or tricking the baby to accept the food you offer, or startling him so that you can shove food in when he drops his jaw in astonishment are the worst things you can do. They are not only cruel, they may eventually yield entrenched resistance and difficulty.

If the baby does begin to respond to your pressure with his own tension, try instead to let him gradually take over his own feeding while you busy yourself in another part of the kitchen. It will get your tension out of the situation until you cool it and let the baby handle his own dilemma. If you continue to press him beyond his interest in food, the backlash will be disproportionate to any gains made. When he becomes more active, he may ruin meals by standing in his chair to show off, ignore his food, beg for pieces of yours, then throw or smash them beyond recognition. Or he may literally cruise around the edge of the table, begging like a troublesome puppy or clawing at whatever he can see. Around twelve months of age he will demonstrate his strong determination to eat what and when he chooses even more resourcefully. He will win, or be completely beaten into uneasy submission. No baby should be allowed to use meals to provoke or heighten tension in his family. If you are clear and firm about what you expect from him and uncompelled by the size of your baby's intake, your baby will learn the social value of mealtime—for you now, and for himself later when he will have to know it.

Between-Meal Snacks

Another not-so-subtle form of pressure is feeding the baby between meals because "he eats so little." It will get you what you may deserve—a child who fusses and picks at his food.

No one needs to feed a baby between meals. According to Dr. Brazelton, one day's nutritional needs are completely met by:

1. A pint of milk (or its equivalent in cheese, ice cream, or a calcium substitute—one teaspoon equals eight ounces of milk).

2. An ounce of fresh fruit juice or one piece of fruit.

3. Two ounces of iron-containing protein, such as one egg or two ounces of meat (one-half jar of baby-food meat or a small hamburger).

4. A multivitamin preparation, which may be unnecesssary but allows you to forget whether your baby has eaten a green, yellow, or *any* vegetable.

These four daily requirements (within a twenty-four-hour period) allow a child normal growth and weight gain. While these requirements may seem extraordinarily simple, no more is necessary, so don't push.

Many mothers feel that as long as they get the food down —even with no holds barred—they have done their duty. Actually mother's responsibility does not end with her baby's last swallow, but with the atmosphere of their feeding exchange.

Dr. Mary D. Ainsworth, a well-known psychologist at The Johns Hopkins University, described how mothers' styles in feeding their babies related to later behavior. Those mothers in her studies who paced the feedings to their babies' wishes, responded promptly to signals of hunger and satisfaction, and allowed their babies to participate actively in the feeding had smooth and mutually gratifying relationships with them. At the end of their first year, these babies showed healthy, undisturbed attachments to their mothers by actively trying to regain contact with them and to maintain it by clinging and resisting release after a brief separation. Babies whose mothers were relatively insensitive and unresponsive to them in feeding situations lacked interest in keeping in touch with them. Or they mixed their efforts at contact with turning, moving, looking away or actually pushing the mothers away. Generally, mothers who could see things from the baby's viewpoint adopted infant-care practices that led to harmonious interaction in feeding and elsewhere. Babies whose mothers consistently and interestingly responded to their behavior learned ways to communicate with the mother other than by hard crying. They could also tolerate frustration better than babies whose behavior made little or no difference in determining what happened to them. Allowing a baby autonomy consistent with his interest and capacity seems to be part of rearing a healthy, happy child.

Motor

Large

Balances head well.

Pushes up on hands and knees and rocks back and forth.
Creeps with object(s) in one or both hands. Goes forward.
May crawl.
May also locomote by raising and lowering buttocks on back, or sitting on side of flexed leg, propelling with corresponding hand and opposite leg.
Helps in being pulled to stand, keeps legs straight.
May pull self to stand.

When supported under arms, stands and bears weight, bounces, steps in place, looks at feet.

Sitting

Sits with slight support.

Sits alone, steadily, several minutes or more, and enjoys it. Balances well.
Hands free while sitting.
Wheels around, leans over.

May get self to sit by pushing up with arms from side, or getting into crawl position and sticking out legs in front.

Small

Thumb apposition complete.
Thumb and fingers grasp block.

Holds two objects, one in each hand, simultaneously. May bang together.

Language

Active

Vowels and consonants occur at random.
Has special, well-defined syllables, usually four or more; most common sound like *ma, mu, da, di, ba.*
Says several sounds in one breath.

Tries to imitate sounds or sound sequences.

May say *dada* and/or *mama.*

Passive

Listens to own vocalizations and those of others.

Please do not regard this chart as a rigid timetable. Babies are unpredictable. Some perform an activity earlier or later than the chart indicates.

Growth Chart

Mental

Attention more concentrated; interested in detail.

Reaches for and grasps toy, like bell or rattle, with one hand. Continues to overextend fingers and concentrate full attention.

Distinguishes near and far objects and space.

Grasps, manipulates, mouths, shakes, bangs object. Plays vigorously with noisemaking toys like bell, music box, or rattle.

Looks briefly for toy that disappears.

Responds with expectation to the repetition of an event or signal. Remembers segment representative of an entire situation. Remembers small series of actions in immediate past if series includes his own actions.

May begin imitating an act.

Continues to compare activities done by one, then the other, side of his body. Visually associates similar acts of his and another person. Responds playfully to mirror image. May associate picture of baby with himself, give appropriate sound.

Interested in consequences of his behavior. But recognizes an event as a goal only after performing the means.

Begins to learn implications of familiar acts. Aware of and compares size differences of similar objects, like blocks.

Transfers object from hand to hand. Retains two of three blocks or small toys offered.

Social

Personal

Reaches and pats mirror image.

Explores body with mouth and hands.

Interaction

May fear strangers.

Begins to show humor. Teases.

Shows desire to be included in social interaction.

Resists pressure to do something he doesn't want to.

Distinguishes friendly and angry talking. May fear performing some familiar activities.

May chew fingers and suck thumb. On back, brings feet to mouth in play. Wriggles in anticipation of play. Plays with toys.

Cultural

Begins finger feeding. Holds and manipulates a spoon or cup in play. Requires independence in feeding.

Stays dry one or two hours.

THE EIGHTH MONTH

Moving Out

THE EIGHTH MONTH
Moving Out

By this time, your baby wil be in perpetual motion when he is awake. He presses forward to new maneuvers, which he joyously combines with his achieved skills. By now he can move well enough to follow you wherever you go. Although he still crawls when he wants to get anywhere quickly, he spends his playtime learning to stand. The baby's steadily increasing ability to get around means that you must strike a balance between containing him and giving him freedom to explore. You must also handle his disinterest in sleep, which limits new and exciting discoveries; understand his fear of strangers; and cope with all the new learning that comes from his added exposure to new sights, sounds and feelings.

Most babies are developing their upright capabilities. If you watch the process carefully, you will see that your baby, while seated, will spread his feet, draw his knees up slightly, and tug on the side of his crib or any other convenient support until he gets into a flexed, half-standing position, his bottom out and wavering. As he gains control of each step in his pull-up, he is free to recognize and use variations. One is a choice between letting go with one or both hands. If he really lets go, he plumps to sitting and has to start again. If he lets go with one hand, he is free to scale his support hand-over-hand. In a day or so, he coordinates the acts of scaling and rising to full height. Then he learns how to gain his balance after leaning against something, to stand, precariously, alone.

He applies little of this experimentation to sitting. He pivots on his bottom until he is dizzy and falls over, but rarely practices at reversing direction. Since he has mastered the basic skill, sitting is fast becoming less exciting than standing.

Being able to stand doesn't mean your baby is going to know how to get down. Most babies spend several painful weeks learning how. Some try falling backward, but since bending as he falls is very difficult for a baby this age to learn, this "solution" is just too painful. Falling backward also triggers the old, disturbing Moro reflex (the startle reflex), which strengthens the baby's inclination to fall straight back with back arched, arms extended, and head and neck thrown back. Although this often means a banged head, infants don't usually hurt themselves in such falls. Fortunately, their skulls are still flexible and cushion the brain so that falls are less likely to produce concussions than they are in adults. Even so, Dr. Brazelton suggests that you put a rug under large pieces of furniture from which your baby could fall.

If your baby continues to have difficulty to get himself down from his new standing position, try to teach him. Stand him at your knees, bend him slightly at the middle, and then gently push him forward and down so that he half-falls into a sitting position. Doing this several times will eventually give him the idea, even though the first daily session, in which he giggles and thoroughly enjoys your instruction, may make you feel he hasn't learned a thing. After a few days, you may be lucky enough to hear or see him practice his new task. When you know he can get himself down, don't cater to his crying for the same assistance at night. The first few times, reteach him just as you did during the day, then let him get to sleep on his own. In a few nights, he will probably stop crying for you.

Although this may seem unnecessarily "disciplinarian," you should not allow his crying at night to continue. Your tension and fatigue will not be much help to you and the rest of the family, and it could spoil your relationship with your baby. He needs the chance to learn about independence from you in small doses.

Life is not all mad activity. More quiet experimentation can busy your eight-month-old for hours. You may have noticed, for example, how much your baby enjoys looking at things upside down. In fact, one way to occupy him on the changing table or in his crib is setting pictures upside down at either end of them. This interest continues into walking, when he will walk with his head thrown back. He may be remembering his usual way of looking at the world many months before when he had to spend so much time on his back. You may also notice your baby sitting and cocking or shaking his head from side to side as he focuses on something in the distance. He is playing with his new awareness that most things keep their size and shape even though his maneuvers,

quick or slow, make an object change perspective. As he recovers his balance, the baby may actually laugh at his ability to change his world.

He will also experiment with his hands. Watch your baby examine any household object you've always taken for granted. He looks at it a long time, feels the surface and edges, turns it upside down and sideways, prods it and drops it just to find out what this three-dimensional object is all about. Putting small blocks or large, colored wooden beads into a large jar, or taking out spools of thread from your sewing box will also fascinate him for hours. He can use either hand. This "pincer" grasp is so new that he practices his holding ability by turning his hands every which way just as he does with other objects of interest. He intently watches his hand as he repeatedly brings thumb and forefinger together. He drops the block on purpose, watches the process, picks it up, drops it—feeling and looking at the new coordination of his muscles. The baby's wonder and delight with his new skill are really appropriate. This separation of thumb and forefinger from the rest of man's "paw" is a great achievement. It allows man a range of manual dexterity from the most delicate sorting of objects to more powerful squeezing or handling of tools. Most eight-month-olds will put down one object before coping with another. But a more precocious eight-month-old may be able to handle two objects simultaneously, pick up one block with one hand, another block with the other, and bang them together zestfully. If he is really advanced, he may even try reaching for a third block with his mouth, or put one of those in his hand into his mouth, and pick up the third with his empty hand.

His intrigue with his prowess means that he may crawl with one hand filled while he explores with the other. It also means he may begin to empty drawers and cupboards, and try tearing things up, including the magazine you haven't read. If your baby manages to acquire a valuable book, don't snatch it away. He may grip it so tightly that you will tear it. Even if this doesn't happen, you will frustrate and bewilder him. Instead, give your baby some magazines of his own to play with. Screen bookcases containing valuable books or art objects with wire mesh when you're not around to protect them. That way he can continue his manual practice, and you can keep your cool, as well as your valuables.

The baby can probably open drawers, too, and one favorite sport may be garnishing the floor with their contents and replacing the original holdings with himself. If you have loop handles on bureaus, dressers, or cupboards, insert a broomstick through them to avoid the inconvenience and mess.

An agile baby is equally able to empty and climb into an older child's toy chest. If it becomes a favorite foray of his, you may have trouble on your hands. The lid can slam over him and trap him inside. Your other child may also rightly resent the invasion of his property. He may fight back, fume helplessly, or if he's especially loving, try teaching his troublesome sib that replacing things can be as much of a game as removing them. As long as he participates, it probably will be enjoyable for the baby. You might help your older child and possibly prevent a tragedy by putting a simple lock that he can open on the chest.

The importance of constant re-evaluation of the dangers a baby can maneuver into during these months of exploration cannot be overstressed. Store and lock away medicines in an unreachable place, and take care of heat sources. No book can enumerate for you the many everyday things and places your particular baby will find enticing targets for exploration. You, as the best judge now of your baby's style and interests, will just have to come up with solutions appropriate to your own home. Weighing real danger against the value of your baby's exploration makes some of these judgments very hard. Freedom to explore speeds learning and achievement. If you keep after your baby constantly to stop his "mistakes" and potential "hurts," you will divert his exercise into a testing of you in each situation. He will be more interested in drawing you into his play than in exploring and learning from his own efforts. Here again your feelings make the difference. Some American mothers do let their babies try things before imposing a "No" because the attempt will help their baby understand, as well as encourage his exploration. Maybe we do demand too much of a baby when we expect him to comprehend "deep" or "hard" or "burning" without having experienced them himself. A burning cigarette may be too fascinating to keep the baby away from until he actually burns himself. Although this method of teaching babies to avoid burning objects has obvious drawbacks, it works. Dr. Brazelton writes, "In the highlands of southern Mexico, an Indian mother never stops her baby as he crawls to the central fire. She says, 'He will learn.' He does and must."

Containing an active child at this stage of life is a difficult task. In desperation or because important household chores are being neglected, most mothers resort to a play-pen. Most such units are devoid of play challenges. The floor area is too small for walking or testing bodily skills. It might be wise to explore the new collapsible fence-type corrals that enlarge play space to four times the traditional playpen. There is on the market an expandable corral that accommodates six changeable play modules in the four sides. Both of these group size units can include visiting babies and serve as a first introduction to peer play.

The Night Watch

Settling down to sleep or quiet times may be equally difficult. Naps may be short and you might have to let the baby give up his morning nap for the single afternoon one. Quiet, sensitive babies, although inactive physically, expend their energy in sorting the kaleidoscope of stimulation they find around them. The sensory and intellectual activity tires them, as does the family hustle and bustle, which is more wearing for them than for more active babies. But an active baby can become so wound up by bedtime that he carries an older child to the point of frenzy with him.

Bedtime is really your decision. It should be handled firmly and with the understanding that few children want to go to sleep. Forcing them to bed may be a relief even to the children because it allows them to quit without losing face. Nothing is as sad as seeing parents wait for their exhausted child to ask for bed. Nine times out of ten, he won't. Children are extraordinarily sensitive to a parent's ambivalence or decisiveness.

Another instance in which you must be decisive is the calling game many babies use when they are at last in bed, and don't want to sleep. Unless a mother is firm, the baby may keep calling as long as anyone comes, or keep throwing his stuffed animal over the side and then wailing for its retrieval. Since words in themselves still mean little at this stage, try telling the baby firmly that enough is enough. Put him on his tummy to show him that you don't consider this a fun game.

If a waking crisis begins to occur, you might try a tech-nique suggested by pediatricians. Before you go to bed rouse, change, cuddle and talk to your baby and give him extra milk when he wants it. During the rest of the night, try to ignore him. He will probably awaken a few more nights.

But if you tell him firmly that it's sleepy time for him, after a week or so, he may need only a pat and change around ten o'clock.

The Universe Is Changing Fast

The eight-month-old's increasing ability to move about offers him new vistas of stimulation. The first signs of imitation indicate that your baby is becoming aware of his humanness and sees the similarities between your body and movements and his. When you put on your coat to go out, he begins to cry. Since this act has been followed by your leaving him in the past, he is cleverly anticipating the same sad event.

Watching you imitate *him* adds new consciousness of his own movements that he loves. A mirror hynotizes him for the same reason. He laughs at the smiling image, pats, and tries to kiss it. He presses his forehead to the mirror to see perhaps if the image is real. He looks at the image of **his** hand and compares it with the real thing, staring at its changing shapes. The sight of his own body movements enhances the kind of perception, called "visuomotor," that your baby needs to learn physical skills.

Mirror play also stimulates awareness of other infants because babies usually watch and imitate each other in preference to strange adults. Perhaps infant observers recognize cues from their own repertoires. This awareness of his identity is probably as thrilling to your baby as a new insight about yourself is to you.

By this time, too, a baby is perfectly able to identify a human face. He is looking for new excitement now. Therefore, he will stare at and attend intently representations of new mental models, especially faces of strangers. Dr. Jerome Kagan of the Harvard Center for Cognitive Studies reports that in a series of experiments with strangers and parents in a room of the baby, a nine-month- to fifteen-month-old begins to show fear when parents leave and the stranger remains. This type of encounter shows the first sign of an infant's ability to hypothesize and *think*.

The baby's ability to form mental models is very important. It has been an accurate indicator of intelligence in later childhood, as measured by the best tests available. This ability starts with mother. Her quick and appropriate response to her baby's signals has been experimentally associated with the baby's rapid building of mental models. Deep, eye-to-eye interaction is a basic of the mother-baby relationship and of building a mental model of the human face. Lack of such interaction may be a primary reason why youngsters in institutions can be retarded mentally and socially, especially in their ability to establish and maintain a close personal relationship, to profit from past mistakes, and to control behavior for future gains.

The baby's better mobility means he can separate himself from you. He realizes this, and the understanding is frightening. He protects himself from this onslaught by turning to you and away from others, and by being especially fussy when you are near. Even a baby who has been very gregarious will show this new dependence. The baby's increased ability to distinguish himself from others, and family members from strangers, only deepens this awareness. From the time the four-month-old becomes more visually aware until twelve months, his acceptance of strangers drops from about four- to one-out-of-five accepts. Withdrawal from strangers—and that usually means anyone beyond the immediate family—peaks in the next few months.

Suddenly the baby has to be held on your lap during your monthly visits to the pediatrician he's "known" for months. He hates to visit, and doesn't want to be left with the sitter he has had since he was two months old. He weeps as if heartbroken as you leave although the sitter reports he starts to play when he realizes you are really gone. If you are torn by your "infidelity," do remember that the baby may not be as disturbed as he pretends. Infants can be great actors.

If your baby anticipates your leaving him with a sitter, he may actually stage spitting up his breakfast a few times— just for effect. Instead of scolding him, cuddle him. Tell him you will miss him a lot; that he will have someone to play with and keep him company; and that you will return and have fun together. While what you say will escape him, the warm contact and familiar voice will reassure and comfort him. Gradually, he may be content when you leave, and turn to his own activities.

During this period, visits by your friends may provoke frantic embraces, howling, or a more subdued refusal to move or to play with his toys. After the door closes at the end of the visit, *then* your child-wonder will start vocalizing and performing gaily.

Try to prepare your baby before going to a strange place. It's the suddenness of a new experience that frightens him, as much as anything else. Most babies need a bit of time to get acquainted with a strange setup, routine, or person, and you can reassure them. If you notice that your baby is afraid of an object, associate it with something pleasant, or look at it, touch it, and handle it together. As you leave home for a visit, talk with him warmly and calmly. Once you arrive, tell your baby repeatedly in a few simple words not to cry, and hold onto him tightly. Suggest to an eager grandparent or aunt not to approach or look at the baby for a little while after arrival, until he approaches them. Looking a baby dead in the eye can build a barrier of wailing as self-protection. Gradual, partial changes are best for a baby, and preparation for the ordeal also helps the relatives. They and other strangers will not feel so bewildered if their eager approaches produce tears and screams, and the baby may soon be able to contain himself to an occasional sob or a stony, anxious silence. Only a well-intentioned chuck under the chin or an over-assertive hug will break his resolve and again produce open sobs. However, by the end of the month, he may sit in a relative's lap, poised if not charmingly expansive. When he successfully keeps his cool, you might try a word of praise. He has taken a giant step in social growth.

At home, you may notice that your baby is more anxious

at certain times, such as right after a nap when he is not fully awake, or when you are too many rooms away from him. When you are safely nearby, your baby crawls around an obstacle, turns to check on you, looks you in the eye, and then smiles. Out of sight, he maintains a flow of chatter. If you move or stop answering, he will scurry right over and bid for some cuddling. This is suddenly serious play. The meaning of separation is apparent, yet the capacity to separate is fragile. You should encourage these experiments as they will reassure your baby and reinforce his ability to explore without fear.

The baby also needs assurance that you will be there when he returns from his excursions, and that you will be there for *him*. If you pick up a friend's baby, and your baby tries to push him out and to climb into your lap, don't tease him. His frantic effort to dislodge a rival is a trauma from which you can spare him. These constant bids may drain you, especially if the baby is your first, or your relationship with him is still a bit uneasy. The dependency of a first child is especially wearing because mother is new to her job, and because there are no sibs to buffer and diffuse the intense relationship. Then, too, mother doesn't have other reasons to spread herself out. Mothers differ also in their acceptance of this behavior according to where they live. Those in large cities are supposedly less tolerant, and push their babies more toward independence. On the other hand, a small apartment only intensifies proximity, and many young mothers find their nerves strung out by day's end. Even so, if you really want to foster the very independence that will free you and your baby, let him cling now instead of shoving him away.

The baby's reactions to relatively insignificant separations and upsets are clues to how he would react to major ones. Babies who have to be hospitalized cling and cry desperately. When they return home, they may also eat and sleep badly, vocalize less, and refuse to be distracted from anxiously scanning their homes.

This prewalking period is no time for any unnecessary separation from you or from familiar surroundings, no matter how short. Dr. John Bowlby, a scientist who has done perhaps the finest research to date on the nature of parent and child attachment says, "The protest, despair and detachment that typically occur when a child over six months is separated from his mother are due to loss of maternal care at this highly dependent, highly vulnerable stage of develop-

ment. The child's hunger for his mother's presence is as great as his hunger for food, and her absence generates a powerful sense of loss and anger."

He adds that the trauma of early loss or separation from the mother can carry over to produce similar responses in older individuals. Such disturbed adults tend to make excessive demands upon others and, if these are not met, to react with anxiety and anger.

A Certain Style

Although motor skills and fear of strangers are more visible this month, your baby is learning in other important areas also. After all, visual and motor exploration leads to greater familiarization with the environment. It gives the context for all later learned or instinctive behavior. One lesson the baby learns now is the basics of quantity. He places one object after another in a bottle, playing with the concept of "more than one." He shakes the bottle with one object in it to make a rattle. Then he shakes it with several as if to hear the difference. He can pick up objects in each hand, bring one to his mouth, then another, then both as if establishing the difference between "each" and "both" with his mouth. He picks up apple chunks with one hand and banana bits with the other, as if sorting their differences by assigning a hand to each.

He is also developing some complex mental skills, perfecting learning methods, and establishing learning styles that will stay with him for years. He is beginning to make associations with things independent of *his* participation. For example, he crawls to the front door when he hears it open because he has associated its opening with arrivals and he is a curious creature. He applies the critical mental power of discrimination to an ever-increasing variety of activities and needs.

As early as the first month, your baby could distinguish your voice and father's. Now as he is mastering standing, he is learning to discriminate between pieces of furniture stable enough to support him and those which will topple with him. At first he may pull over anything, his sister's doll table, sofa pillows, or blankets, and fall backward. But after the first trials and errors, he gradually settles down to a few favorite, sturdy spots to which he returns for his daily pull-ups.

His discriminatory power may also serve a real noisemaking urge. First he learns, perhaps accidentally, that if he bangs his hands flat on a table top he makes a loud thumping noise. He tries it on any table he finds. Then he figures out that some tables make more noise. He learns that a table full of china rattles especially, so he rushes to the breakfast table after you take him out of his bounce chair. If you doubt that he has associated table and china with more and more intriguing noise, watch his face one morning when you've already removed the cups and saucers.

At this stage, your baby develops some complex mental skills, including memory of timing and "gestalt." By gestalt we mean a mental perception of the whole without emphasis on individual parts. For example, if your baby likes to explore rooms, you may notice that a displaced coffee table or a new object gracing the end table attracts him immediately. His memory of the entire scene, or the "gestalt," fixed in this case by his last sight of the room, frees him to efficiently select the new, or discrepant, piece. If your other babies weren't as persistent or alert to detail, this one may surprise you so much at first that the cocktail glasses left from last evening's company may tumble to his charge.

He is also developing a memory of timing. He may terminate a particularly awful feeding by judiciously dropping his cup overboard. As he releases it, he blinks his eyes in delicious anticipation of the cup's crash. He has become conscious of the time interval before contact. In the evening he crawls to the front door to greet his father even before it opens. This may be a first example of your baby's ability to recall a past *event* rather than a past action of his own. His new sense of timing leads him to expect an important, regular event.

One learning method we all use is to push around our "knowns" until they form a new pattern. The baby does this very early when he climbs. Scaling mammals learn to climb instinctively and unconsciously simply by joining reflexes appropriate and ready for climbing. Although our infants inherit some instinctive urge to climb, the several skills needed for it are *learned* and first used for activities that have nothing to do with climbing. To climb, the baby consciously borrows a known technique here and another there, and eventually puts them together in one smooth performance. First he gives up a two-handed grasp in favor of alternating hands. Then he adds a flexing and straightening of his body to scale upward. He learns to put together segments of a whole action with remarkable speed.

The ways babies put together these basic learning methods to acquire mental skills is as much a part of a personal style as the way each moves. In experiments with one- to ten-month-old babies at Harvard's Center for Cognitive Studies, faces and balls appeared briefly in each of two windows. Some babies found the faces more interesting; some, the balls. Others were equally attracted by both. Reports from mothers suggest that, in some cases at least, those who prefer the balls are happier when playing with objects and toys; those who prefer the faces are happier in social interactions.

Some babies will not be pressured to perform before they are ready. This stubborn determination is a kind of strength. Some babies operate with a master plan for reaching their goal. They learn maneuvers separately and put them together deliberately toward an end result. They react more to a situation as a whole. Others have a roster of skills that they sample until they find what works for them. Both types may practice until their self-assigned tasks become "easy"—a quality of persistence essential in moving toward a goal. Still others prefer to manipulate people in their environment instead of working with their own accomplishments. An only child with hovering parents may already know how to play helpless. As a tot, he may continue to point to things instead of naming them because mother has always been his interpreter. The baby may habitually refuse to get his own toys because you have always gotten them. If you notice a clue like this, try some judicious inattention. If you can, get your baby to give up this learning approach. It is probably not rigidly fixed yet.

Constructive molding and teaching imply mother's appreciation of her baby's learning pace and style. As the late Dr. Lawrence K. Frank of the Macy Foundation put it, "Children have different cognitive styles, their own individual ways of perceiving and understanding the world, some visual, others auditory, while others prefer to deal with the world as it can be directly manipulated and felt. Various studies today, including accumulating clinical evidence, are showing that once a perceptual style has been developed it resists modification or replacement."

Motor

Large

Pivots on tummy.
Crawls. May go forward or
backward at first.
May crawl with one hand full.
May also go forward by sitting and
bouncing on buttocks, or by
standing, lunging, and grabbing at
furniture.

Stands leaning against something,
hands free.
Pulls on furniture to stand.
Needs help to get down from
standing.
May stand holding on to hand.
Held standing, puts one foot in
front of the other.

Sitting

Sits alone steadily for several
minutes, one leg stretched out in
front, the other flexed.
Sits and bounces on buttocks.

Gets self to sit. Pushes up with
arms from side. Or in crawl
position, flexes one leg to tummy,
extends and pushes it against
surface, other leg follows.

Small

Thumb, first and second fingers
grasp block.
Has pincer grasp, thumb and
forefinger.
Tries to pick up pellet; rakes.
Picks up string.
Grasps partially with fingers.

Holds rattle for at least three
minutes.

Reaches for objects with fingers
overextended. Must pay full
attention.

Language

Active

Babbles with variety of sounds
and inflections, spontaneously,
for fun, or alone; still primarily
for self.
Imposes adult intonation on
babbling.
Shouts.

Vocalizes satisfaction.

Begins to mimic mouth and jaw
movements.

Uses two-syllable utterances.
May label an object in imitation
of its sound, e.g., train, *choo-choo*.
May say *dada* and/or *mama*
as specific names.

Passive

Usually responds, e.g., turns head
and torso, to familiar sounds
nearby: his name, the telephone,
vacuum cleaner.
Listens selectively to familiar
words. Begins to recognize
some.

Please do not regard this chart as a rigid timetable. Babies are unpredictable. Some perform an activity earlier or later than the chart indicates.

Growth Chart

Mental

Reacts promptly to situation.

Examines objects as external, three-dimensional realities. Watches hands in various positions, holding, and dropping objects. Explores notions of "in" and "out," "container-contained," by putting small objects in and out of jar.

Searches behind a screen for an object if he is looking at it as it is hidden. Only conceives of object in place where it first appears.

Recalls past event as well as a past action of his own. Retains small series of events in immediate past without his own action.

Anticipates events independent of his own behavior. Begins showing memory of timing; memory of "gestalt."

Has mental model of the human face; grows interested in variations of the model.

Begins imitating people and behaviors out of sight and earshot.

Aware of the relation between his body and movements, and those of others.

Subordinates means to goal. Solves simple problems. Kicks at hanging toy to try to get it. Rings bell purposefully. Pulls string to secure attached toy.

Holds and manipulates one object, like block, and regards second type of object, like a cup. May attempt to secure three blocks.

Begins establishing differences between each and both; and between one and more-than-one.

Begins establishing a learning style. Begins using learning techniques. Combines known bits of behavior into a new act.

Social

Personal

Pats, smiles at, tries to kiss mirror image.

Interaction

Fears strangers.
Is clearly attached to mother. Approaches and follows her Fears their separation. Usually awakens or quiets when mother talks to him.

Shouts for attention.

Pushes away something he doesn't want. Rejects confinement.

May know how to use parents to get things for him.

Reaches persistently for toys beyond reach. Bites, chews them. Sustains interest in play.

Cultural

May have trouble sleeping.

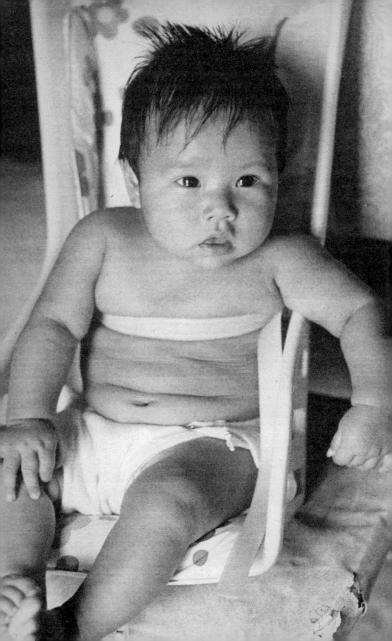

THE NINTH MONTH
Upright and Feeling Down

THE NINTH MONTH
Upright and Feeling Down

After the tremendous surge of activity in the seventh and eighth months, when your baby perfected his sitting and crawling abilities and began to stand, the ninth month is a temporary slack. The baby uses this period before he walks to secure his impressive gains, to practice mental skills, and acquire some social arts. He settles on a definite crawling style, and his speed improves. When the telephone rings he can beat you to it and will listen patiently to the perplexed voice at the other end of the line before you arrive. He is also diverted by just lifting the receiver and listening to the series of developing sounds.

He polishes his sitting performance by rolling smoothly to his side, subtly shifting balance, and continuing on up to sit. Many babies will also sit by getting into a crawl position, flopping back on their bottoms, and bringing their legs out in front. Some babies will get themselves to sit in both ways before settling on one.

The baby's memory and other mental capabilities also improve. In experimental environments, nine-month-olds clearly become bored with, in fact plainly dislike, repetitions of the same stimulation. Younger babies fail to grow bored because each presentation is novel. A nine-month-old can remember a game he's been playing with his sibs the evening before, and will try to get them back to it in the morning. His memory of his pediatrician's office after several months' absence demonstrates recall in an even more important situation. He can now fully conceive of some objects as independent of his ego.

If he can move to a place with one toy, then return repeatedly to get others for his play, he is able to keep a series of ideas in mind. This ability to attend to and use several ideas at once is an important mental skill.

When he can build a small tower of two or three blocks, he is learning more about quantity and the concept of things in a series. He is also acquiring persistence. Without this ability to keep at something until it is done, bursts of artistic inspiration, no matter how brilliant, seldom become achievements for others to enjoy. Equally marvelous is the muscular control necessary to grasp a block with a two-finger grasp, pick it up, convey it to another block, and align the two so they will not topple.

Don't be disturbed if your baby doesn't match these descriptions. Many babies about nine months old, especially very active and very quiet ones, may be devoting themselves to other very different learning tasks. This is perfectly fine and suited to their own growing pace. Differences among babies will be more pronounced now than they were during the first six months of life, when the baby's brain and nervous system were changing more dramatically and his reflexes were more in control of his movements.

A quiet baby may spend part of his day unobtrusively experimenting with all aspects of sitting. He may even propel himself sitting on the side of one leg bent at the knee, pulling with the arm on the same side, and pushing with the foot on the opposite side. This new way to get about may replace his slower belly flops, and his speed increases slowly. In his stroller or walker, he is content to sit and make changes in his visual world by covering his eyes or bending his head at different angles.

By contrast many a baby may actually stand alone, unsupported. Letting go of his familiar supports, he daringly totters from one leg to the other. A baby often grows quite enamored of a big developmental step such as this. His relentless practice often means that he will greet any limitations of it, including sleep, with resistance. You may have to cut out a nap and try to dress and feed your baby as he stands if he is really insistent. The baby, sitting, crawling or standing, is now likely to be anywhere in the house, so calling to see where he might be hidden becomes *de rigeur.* In the space of a week or so, an active baby may learn to push himself up from his tummy with both arms, place one foot and then the other on the floor, straighten his legs and arms, and come to stand *by himself* by lifting his trunk and using his waist as a pivot. He may stop the action at one point in the routine and crawl like a spindly daddy longlegs, bottom high in the air, on his straightened arms and legs.

A very active baby may even want to take steps holding

onto your hands, or actually lunge from wall to wall or furniture in his desperation to get moving. This month may also find him trying out his crawling prowess on the stairs, so you must either teach him how to back down safely if he doesn't figure it out himself or make the stairs off-limits.

A New World

With the ability to stand comes a price tag of insecurity and the job of reappraising old skills that suddenly have other dimensions and new implications. The baby becomes aware of vertical spaces as he climbs up and down from heights posed by chairs and stairs.

He also learns a sense of space from using his hands more and more efficiently. He begins to accommodate his hands to the shape of what he is reaching for. He grabs for a large, round object with both hands as if he knows he needs both to hold it. He turns his hand so that he can pick up a pencil along its long dimension.

He is suddenly afraid to budge from chairs he has climbed from many times before, and he may be concerned about as simple a thing as the vacuum cleaner. When you turn it on, he cries miserably in a corner. Since he is probably intrigued as well as terrified, leaving him in another room is no answer. Instead, hold him close with one hand while you vacuum with the other and calmly say something like "It won't hurt you." When the vacuum is turned off, encourage him to touch and explore it. Gradually the baby will conquer this dread, too, and play comfortably as you work. Another new fear may be the bathtub. He may have been playing in it for months, yet now he whimpers pitifully during his bath and clutches the tub-side passionately. Bathe him in his old bathinette if it makes him happier, or bathe him with you in the tub, holding him close as you lower him. He will slowly regain his old confidence and in a month or so feel up to taking a bath alone again.

He may also have trouble getting along with his brothers and sisters. Babies, even those used to fielding the noise and commotion of sibs, show increased sensitivity to children during this period. Their vigorous, unpredictable movements and sounds are just too much to tolerate as the baby conquers new fears and insecurities.

Even though sibs may seem an added hardship during this period of readjustment, the baby's constant work and interest in mastering all that happens around him attest to the worth of a stimulating environment. A baby who sees few children besides a brother or sister is especially sensitive to other children now. An only child may be so unused to them that he stares uncooperatively as they play nearby, jumps if they move or shout suddenly, or shrinks away fearfully if they approach him. This kind of baby actually needs more contact with children to overcome his sensitivity. A baby *is* more interested in watching children than adults, and babies in preference to older children. If your baby is socially inexperienced, allow him to take in his universe slowly. Two or three active youngsters in his own house at the same time may present too big a slice of life at this stage of his growth.

Mothers' Help

Mothers react differently to a baby's fear. Some mothers over-react and are too protective. Others push too hard and even resent the baby's old attachments. Mothers with more than one child are particularly prone to this. Suddenly aware of something about the baby they think needs attention, their guilt about imagined neglect pushes them. For example, all the babies in the neighborhood are using a cup by now, so mother grows exasperated at her baby's clumsiness and determines to wean him from his bottle with which he is content. Some of her neighbors agree with her. The baby, however, resists these efforts. The more she presses, the more determined he becomes. When she "cons" him with flavoring, he drinks milk from his cup, but when she phases out the flavoring, he balks again. The baby may čue her to his feelings in other ways. Milk from the cup rolls down his face while orange juice, for instance, is swallowed neatly.

Try imitation to teach your baby to manipulate and drink from his cup. Give the baby a cup while you use one. Then give him some milk to experiment with. Let him play with his cup in the bathtub where he cannot create a mess, even if he does sample the bath water, too. If you make using a cup a game, the baby will learn how to use it unaware, and the real transition from bottle to cup will be less painful.

Appropriate comfort and reinforcement are most important during this stage of your child's life, but they are not easy. Each incident demands an on-the-spot evaluation and a prompt response. You can probably hearten a baby more easily with a kind word and a gentle squeeze if you respond

to his cry immediately. He is more likely to dissolve into a quivering heap of self-pity if you wait too long.

Another way to help is to turn a fear into a positive experience. A baby may be in such a hurry as he crawls that he gets ahead of himself and splatters forward on his nose. His pained look may reflect more surprise at his predicament than real hurt. You can boost his morale with a quick hug or a sympathetic pat on the back, and by calmly setting him straight again. Short and sweet, these boosts might do better than prolonged expressions of sympathy. With prompting from a few minor accidents at which you laugh, the baby may sprawl deliberately on his tummy and face, and squirm with laughter—strictly for your benefit. Your amusement encourages his budding sense of humor.

Showing, Shaping, and Shoving

Because your baby is becoming more and more of an individual in the ways he does things, your help and intervention should accordingly become more specialized. Dr. Gewirtz says that many parents do not understand the importance of the circumstances in which such things as food and love are provided, particularly as these circumstances relate to the baby's behavior. According to the latest annual report from Harvard's Center for Cognitive Studies, clumsy intervention that violates the child's cycle of effort and pause can bring frustration, failure, and tears. Harvard researchers asked mothers to help their six-month-olds fetch a toy from behind a transparent screen. Since babies this age do not solve this task spontaneously, the mother's style of assistance was important. Kenneth Kaye, who conducted the research, picturesquely calls the three teaching techniques he distinguished, "showing, shaping, and shoving." In the first, the mother shows the baby what to do. He found that mothers do this when they believe, rightly or wrongly, that the baby can organize a comparable act although the baby may not have shown that he could do more than parts of it. "Shoving" was literally guiding or pushing the baby's hand. It grew from the mother's conviction that the infant already knew how to do the job well. "Shaping," the most sophisticated teaching method, involved breaking down the act into more manageable segments, the basic idea behind programmed learning. For example, the mother first moved the toy to the edge of the screen so the baby could reach and grab, minus the difficult cues of transparent materials and the complicated problem of hooking his hand behind something. Mothers used this modeling technique when they felt the baby was not quite up to the task. Wrongly applied, each teaching technique led the baby to resist, avert his eyes, and to break off the learning exchange with his mother. Appropriately applied, each technique was successful. One critical requirement for success was the mother's timing so that her teaching occurred during the natural breaks in the baby's activity. Another was the mother's correct judgment of her baby's cues. For example, a mother could think her baby able to do a task when in fact he was not up to it and, therefore, would shove him rather than shape his behavior.

Generally, a mother's teaching should grace the baby's readiness for a learning task and aim to support his self-realization, neither ignoring nor overwhelming it. The baby will add voluntary mastery to his system of reflexes, at a time when freedom and exploration can characterize his achievements. Then a baby can refuse as well as accept what he is about to internalize. When he can accept it, he experiences the sheer joy of learning that will enrapture you when your baby first walks. These feelings are reason enough. But additional bonuses in this teaching style are the greater stability of the behavior itself, easier teaching, and your satisfaction in teaching successfully.

Self-Help

Besides your intervention, the baby himself will try to cope. He may act out some of his new fears, experiences, and

goals. If you look for them, you will see these precious bits of play and practice. For example, he may try to allay his anxiety about heights by repeatedly standing, then purposely falling to his knees or bottom. He may crawl up a few stairs, drop his favorite stuffed animal down them, then back down to the bottom, pick it up, and console it. This is an early sign of symbolic thought. The baby has clearly recorded a situation in his mind so effectively that he can "put it on" to something else. For example, after a trauma like hospital-ization or even a visit to the dentist, an older child will often ease its scars with play, repeatedly acting out bits and pieces of the experience. If you feel your child needs it, you can even set up a play situation aimed at a difficult episode or an old fear.

With such "self-help," this period is bound to pass. While the baby's fears lead to a temporarily greater need for his mother, they also foretell bursts of independence and growth. They signal that he is consolidating tenuous "feelers" and gathering security from the physical world—and you—before trying new exploits.

There is little real need for friends' advice to determine your handling of your baby. You know yourself and your baby better than anyone else. Sometimes even well-intentioned people are just plain wrong. As Dr. Gewirtz writes, "A parent labeled loving by his community might dispense stimulation which would appear to him and it to indicate love and attentive care, but which may have little or no effect on his child's behavior. On the other hand, the apparently indifferent parent may respond sparingly to his child but the stimulation provided could suit and encourage the child's learning."

We all seem to make the general mistake of equating suc-cessful mothering with the child's speed in growing up. Hopefully today's generation of young parents will understand more fully that a wiser aim is soundness, not speed, for each step of child-rearing, and that "doing your own thing" is better than worrying about other people's opinions.

A Proper Person

The time when your baby learns to stand and walk is a common second peak for sibling rivalry. The baby is better able to get in his sib's way and he is becoming a personal threat as well. Just as you could not trust your toddler's feelings during the previous period, you cannot now, especially since his own interim learning may inspire him to even more sophisticated torture methods.

Rivalry between a baby and a toddler can be suppressed or quite visible. You may become aware that your three-year-old is feeding the baby a varied menu of leftovers, birdseed and aspirin that he wouldn't dare eat himself. These clandestine feedings represent a mixture of unconscious emotions and deliberate intent. Unknowingly, he may even wish to hurt him.

Your toddler may also intervene directly to counter an act that threatens him. As the baby makes a play for your husband at day's end, your three-year-old butts in and roars to drown out the baby's greetings. Or, realizing how precarious the baby's new standing skill is, your three-year-old skims past him, whirls, and charges during the baby's exercise sessions. The baby falls or grabs that table he's been smart enough to stand close to. Littering the floor around the baby, yelling, or slamming doors—preferably in his face—are other harassments that stem from jealousy.

This unsettling influence retards the standing and walking of many second or third children. Luckily, however, the environment is not wholly responsible for a baby's learning, and baby's inner drive is very strong.

While the baby practices his physical accomplishments, he learns to protect himself and his possessions from a marauder. He begins to gather toys in his lap and hover over them during his brother's bad moods. In the evenings, when his brother sweeps past him to his father, shoving him in the rush, he flattens to his tummy, hands over his lowered head. He becomes sensitive to his brother's anger and learns to differentiate it from the less dangerous anger of others. He knows when and how long to play quietly in a protected nook or near another family member. And he also grows sensitive to the controls older family members exercise to reduce his danger.

Even though your children's tensions and ugly emotions can be very difficult to handle, fighting has a certain value. Children really enjoy many of their squabbles and fights. When else in their lives will they ever be allowed to release anger so directly? More important, they, like adults, sometimes need to express the ugly side of a relationship to free positive feelings for each other.

The baby learns more from his sibs than the arts of protecting himself and evaluating people's moods and motives. He learns how to cooperate and to live with others.

Games, like sports later on, are good outlets for the aggressive, competitive facets of their relationship, as well as a way to learn teamwork. Your baby's wish to appeal to his sib sparks a game of catch. Although he can't really get a ball back to his teammate, he does grasp it with one, then two hands, and pushes it out and drops it as if he understands the process. His aim is hardly an asset either, but his brother's pleasure in throwing to the baby motivates him to run and pick up the ball for him. Another ballgame can involve throwing a toy for the baby to fetch, even if it also includes grabbing the toy from the baby's hand. A mother should encourage rather than interrupt these healthy exchanges among her children. Dashing to safeguard your baby's right to the retrieved object will only make your two-year-old feel guilty for having snatched it, spoil a valuable exercise, and cast it in another light for both. As is, the game satisfies your baby's love of action and reconciles your toddler's conflicting feelings toward his younger sib.

Babies learn still more from brothers and sisters. Their make-believe tea parties foster the baby's dexterity as he holds his hands and cup in readiness for the promised tea. He learns the social nature of mealtimes. If you give your children a little milk in their cups, your baby may actually learn to drink from a cup during this play.

An older sister and her baby brother may look at picture books and magazines together, if she enjoys them. She may try reading to the baby, who unappreciatively snares the pages and rips them as he tries to turn them too. As your tot murmurs lengthy sentences in imitation of you, she moos for the cows, meows for the kittens and labels them all. Besides the togetherness, this is valuable language practice for toddler and baby alike.

The relationship among sibs, despite troubled times, is too valuable to sacrifice to your fears of letting them work out their struggles. Unfortunately, many parents feel that after a toddler has won the first round against negative feelings, a rematch is out of order. This reaction only drives hostility underground and makes the older child miserable and possibly even more determined to undermine the baby. These parental expectations are unfair, too, because competitive, selfish feelings are never completely controlled in adults, let alone in children.

Besides, even at nine months of age, the baby himself is not as helpless as he may seem. As long ago as the 1930s, John Watson, one of the first developmental psychologists interested in babies, researched the way infants played with their contemporaries at different age levels during the first year. Before four or five months, he says, babies hardly seek social contact with other babies although social relationships with adults are already forming. At about five months, one baby will smile to another or cry if another receives attention. But these are courtesy gestures, still removed from real social exchange. Watson put babies six months and over in playpens with toys—hollow cubes, drums and drumsticks, and balls, which the babies were shown how to roll back and forth to each other.

Babies six to eight months old often paid more attention to their surroundings than to the toys or their playmates. When one baby tried to be sociable, the other often ignored him. Friendly contacts, when they did occur, were awkward, almost bashful, and limited to looks, smiles, and mutual grasping. Games were few and short, often consisting of the babies' unspecific handling of the same object. Fights were equally impersonal, more like blind attempts to get hold of the toys. In contrast, babies nine to thirteen months old responded quickly to the toys. But they were hardly sociable creatures. Since their playmates often became an obstacle to getting them, personalized fighting was at its maximum during these months.

Along with this intensified fighting, your children will come to find more genuine pleasure in each other. Although your older child may be openly antagonistic and competitive as the baby guards himself and his toys, he also begins to respect him as a person for they have begun to play as equals.

Motor

Large

Crawls with one hand full.
Can turn around.
May crawl upstairs.
May crawl on straightened limbs.

Stands briefly with hand held.
May stand alone briefly.
May get self to stand without pulling up on furniture.
Gets down from standing.
May side-step or "cruise" along furniture.

Sitting

Sits well in chair.
Sits steadily and indefinitely alone.
Pivots 90 degrees seated.

Gets self to sit effortlessly.

May learn to sit down from standing.

Small

Successfully grasps pellet or shoe-laces with thumb and forefinger.

Clasps hands or bangs objects together at center of body.

Index finger begins to lead, points, tries to poke into holes, hooks and pulls.

May build tower of two blocks.

Language

Active

Intonation patterns become distinct.

Signals emphasis and emotions by vocalizing.

Imitates coughs, tongue clicks, hisses.

Uses words meaningfully, says *dada* and/or *mama* as specific names.
May say a syllable or a longer sequence repeatedly.

Passive

Listens to conversations, singing tones.
May understand and respond to one or two words other than name, like *no-no*.
May carry out simple commands, pleased with his understanding; e.g., "Go get my slippers."

Please do not regard this chart as a rigid timetable. Babies are unpredictable. Some perform an activity earlier or later than the chart indicates.

Growth Chart

Mental

Fears heights. Aware of vertical space.
Recognizes dimensions of objects.
Approaches small object with finger and thumb, large object with both hands.
Changes dimensions of objects by partially covering eyes or looking upside down.

Fingers holes in pegboard.

Uncovers toy he has seen hidden.

Grows bored with repetition of same stimuli.
May remember a game from previous day.
Anticipates reward for successful completion of act or command.
Anticipates return of person or thing he has released manually or visually.

Watches scribbling intently.

Can keep a series of ideas in mind.

Picks up and manipulates two objects, one with each hand. Hits or pushes objects against each other.
Drops one of two blocks to get a third. May put one of two objects in mouth and get a third.

Role-plays troublesome acts, shows symbolic thinking.

May refuse to allow self to be distracted. May begin showing quality of persistence.

Social

Personal

Recognizes mother and self in mirror.
Perceives mother as separate person; father, probably.

Interaction

Anticipates mother coming for feeding.

Performs for home audience.
Repeats act if applauded.

May learn to protect self and possessions, fight for disputed toy.
May be more sensitive to other children, cries if they cry.
Begins to evaluate people's moods and motives.

May play out new fears.
Shows interest in other people's play.
Initiates play.
Plays pat-a-cake, so-big, bye-bye, and ball games.
Chooses toy deliberately.

Cultural

Feeds self cracker. Holds bottle.
Uses cup handle. Manipulates and drinks from cup.

May fear bath.

THE
TENTH
MONTH
Imagination

THE
TENTH
MONTH
Imagination

In the next several months, your baby will work on putting his world in motion. Unless he is very active, his slowdown in motor learning will very likely continue this month but the lull is deceptive, for he is really gathering strength to carry him through that big step of walking. This month, however, he will expend some of his energy on improving old skills, but he will devote more and more of it to social and personal growth.

He can finger feed so well now that he can feed himself an entire meal. He is very insistent on feeding himself, although he may still allow you to feed him mushy foods with a spoon. If he has sibs, he will try to keep up and eat with them—the same food, please, in bite size.

He smoothes rough edges off the motions of sitting, crawling and standing he has so recently and relentlessly learned. He may even get himself to stand by straightening his four limbs from a crawl position, pushing off with his palms, and lifting the weight of his trunk. Standing, he may practice stepping sideways facing a couch. At first hesitant, he "cruises" more and more easily and quickly. Speeding along, he slides one foot after the other, his hands barely skimming the surface of the couch seat. When he learns to walk, he will lose this ability. Keep in mind that many babies, particularly heavy ones, will cruise later, and some never experiment with cruising or standing. They just seem to wait until they can get up and walk.

Cautious about heights in the month before, a ten-month-old dares to climb from a chair now, but still scrupulously surveys the distance. Babies at this age still distrust their visual cues. Brazelton says, "those who want to slide off an unfamiliar changing table will drop their legs over first to test the space and cling to their support until they feel the ground below." If they can't find it, they scramble up onto the table again. This caution is absent in babies who are hurtlers, but more cautious infants show a respect for heights.

New skills your baby probably will work on are manual, perhaps carrying two small objects in one hand across a room to their container. You may also notice that your baby is beginning to separate the assignments of each hand—the left for carrying and the right for manipulating, if he is "right-handed." Seated, he sucks his left thumb but frees his right for play and exploration. The reduction of the left hand to container and carrier enforces the increasing emphasis and dexterity of the right hand, and begins differentiating active and passive sides of the body. The baby might also be ready to learn the subtleties of pushing an object to one side instead of shoving it forward and backward, his natural style of pushing. Try working with him on a merry-go-round toy. Besides pushing differently, he will also have to discover how and when to let go.

A Late Weaning Means Catching Up

Unlike most babies, a quiet baby may show a long-awaited spurt in motor activity this month. For a quiet baby who may still be nursing, this late spurt in development may prompt a weaning. Physical progress and refusing the breast are often more than coincident. At this time, the baby may wean himself very simply, and much more easily than you can. One day, perhaps after a particularly large dose of milk from his cup, he will just avert his face and push your breast with the flat of his hand. There is no denying the meaning of this cue. You shouldn't feel rejected or angry or guilty when your baby first refuses your breast. Your baby may almost imperceptibly show you in other ways that he misses the closeness of nursing times.

You need not worry that you have been constraining your baby's development by nursing him so long. Even though many babies seem swathed in a gentle cocoon during nursing, this period allows the baby to store energy and experience that far outweigh any delay. Maturation of the nervous system doesn't stop in the cocoon. It continues on to certain necessary minimum levels of maturity that allow major developmental events to occur. A three-month-old baby, for example, simply has not reached the minimum level of maturity and muscular control for holding a marble between his thumb and forefinger. When an infant reaches the appropriate stage for a given development, such as sitting up alone, it gets done with very little practice. Children hospitalized with body casts who have never walked can walk within a few days after the casts are off if they have reached the appropriate stage of maturation.

Very quickly, your baby will sit alone, stand and crawl. He can now sit with a straight back and pivot 90 degrees if he wants to reach for or look at something behind him. His thumbsucking and sitting will quickly yield to crawling and standing, as if he feels a new freedom at last. Since some quiet babies require a little more encouragement, you may teach yours to stand by firmly refusing to give him a favorite toy you are holding even though he points and calls for it. The incentive of frustration may finally make him creep to you, pull on your legs, grab for your out-stretched hands, and pull up, though he may still whimper to be let down. Heartened by his standing successes, he may also begin to crawl. Once he gets going, you may see him head toward a corner to curl into or a chair to huddle under. There he turns to survey the room he has just conquered. Since he doesn't know how to crawl backward yet, you may sometimes have to extract him from between pieces of furniture or from between wall and loveseat, where he is firmly wedged, wailing.

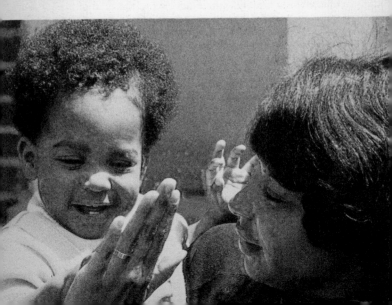

Despite this inconvenience and his laborious style, the sight of your baby moving may seem more gratifying than anything you've felt in a long time. Even though he is crawling and standing with support at ten months, in comparison to the "average" baby at eight months, and a precocious one at seven, remember that he has put three major acts together—sitting, crawling and standing—in about half the time. He is on his own personal timetable of sturdy development.

In sharp contrast, an active baby may pass most of his time on his feet and protest lying down. A very active baby may even be learning to walk. You will find on your next trip to your pediatrician that all this standing has made the baby lose about an inch of his height. Actually the vertebrae in his backbone have settled. Even adults measure an inch shorter normally than they would if they were bedridden—a small price for being upright.

Tension is often the companion of bursts of physical activity, and this can mean sleeping problems. But unlike earlier periods of unrest, your baby, now physically stronger, can rock his crib on hands and knees and make a racket loud enough to rouse the entire household. You will help everyone concerned by helping the baby with his sleeping problem. Try a little after-dark communion in which you rock and croon to him, and feed him close to you until you feel him begin to let go. It will help him stay asleep later.

A Sense of Identity

During these next couple of months, many babies concentrate on the interaction between their emerging personalities and their families. Your baby will show many real moods and emotions now, and grow more and more self-conscious and aware of social approval and disapproval.

As you know, your baby's crying was his earliest and most easily identifiable emotional response. One reason the baby learned to cry was to signal for your help with his pain or discomfort. But he often cried just to relieve internal pressure, as all advocates of "a good cry" already know. Although he still cries for these reasons, he does so less often. Most likely your baby cries now because of his fear of strange people, places, and activities, or his unhappiness at being separated from you and other loved ones. Even emotional separations, such as the aftermath of a scolding, can make him look sad and hurt. He can sit daydreaming as if he has much to contemplate. He can also grow angry, especially when you frustrate an activity he feels is important. Just like adults, babies get angry more often when they are tired, hungry, or physically not up to snuff. Just like adults, they are more content when they are rested, healthy, and well-fed. Your baby's laughter and joy are a delight to the whole family. He shows his pleasure when father comes home in the evening, and he licks his lips in satisfaction at a good meal. He may begin to enjoy music. A familiar tune can set him rocking as he pats his hands and hums along.

Your baby probably extends his tenderness now to stuffed animals and other toys. The capacity to love or mother something is a real compliment to you, for it can only come from the experience of being lovingly and happily mothered.

The baby also grows sensitive to social approval, partly because of his new awareness that mother and father are humans separate from himself. He can begin to infer something about his mother's goals for him and about the plans she is adopting to achieve them. Then he can try to accommodate them and win approval, or alter her goals toward his wishes through gentle persuasion or obstinate refusal.

Most babies this age will not show off their latest accomplishments away from home. Depending on his personality, your baby may relish or feel quite shy about performing for a family audience. Capitalizing on his performing arts, his sibs may make him a willing mouthpiece. After he has learned a new word or gesture, your baby may spend days rehearsing it and offering it to every one of your questions. Soon the word loses meaning and appropriateness. It becomes a companion of play, a sound to fill in silence, or a ploy to attract your attention. It lasts as a focal point in time and space as long as you react. When he senses you are growing bored, your baby will discard the mangled word and move on to a new one. In this way, he learns to "look sad," to "snuggle and kiss," and to say "bye-bye," waving as you leave the room or house, and giggling and clapping when you return.

On the other hand, your baby may be suspicious of your teasing him. Although he may eventually gain enough confidence to perform at your knee, his attempts are still very fragile. If you laugh, catch his eye, join in the funny little croaks that sometimes sound like a singer's crooning, or try to show him off for anyone else, he stops the recital.

He is also beginning to say "No." Sometimes he accompanies his refusals with a wag of his head. Don't immediately assume the baby is being difficult. Even though he can balk when he wants to, the baby probably has only a vague sense of what the word "No" is all about. Besides, the most natural movement of the head is from side to side, something the baby has been doing since he was a week old when he followed moving objects with his eyes. So he will learn this gesture more quickly than the nod that goes with "Yes."

During this emotional growth, the baby is developing his sense of identity about himself and what belongs to him. He may grow disinterested in his sister's toys and play more with his own. He may even be able to sort his own toys from a jumble in the nursery.

His first reactions to himself were probably long-ago percepts of his own body. He heard his own cry, felt his body moving, saw and manipulated his own fingers and toes. Later he learns to recognize his own voice or touch or face as different from those of others. Maybe as late as two years of age, children have some grasp of the total self-unity. At this age, when you ask him, "Where are your —————?" he can point to his teeth, eyes, ears, hair, and toes. You might begin the game by pointing to and naming each part of a favorite doll. Then, as you label, your baby learns to point. After several rounds, you ask the baby where his eyes are. He may be able to point correctly. The ability to extrapolate from the doll to himself is a big step. It means the baby has recognized the doll as an inanimate object in front of—that is, separate—from him, yet with certain clear similarities to his own body parts. If you ask him to point to *your* eyes or nose or mouth, he may show he understands your request by looking at the right feature but turning away, chagrined. Don't be too disappointed at the refusal; his behavior might mean that he recognizes how different you are from him and his doll. Some babies, on the other hand, do better starting with mother's or a family member's features.

Babies may also start to evolve a sexual identity. Baby boys and girls have differed importantly much earlier than this. Girls are much more consistent in their behavior than boys are, and are generally much more attentive. They are usually more precocious in their development, and are more intrigued with novelty. They also talk more. In experimental situations, baby girls as young as six months of age paid more

attention to male than female faces while their male contemporaries attended more to pictures of females. Now the
differences are even more apparent.

Sexual identity probably begins as simple imitation, but is
so strongly encouraged by both parents alike that they contribute to its growth. Dr. Howard A. Moss of the National
Institute of Health has established experimentally what many
social scientists have known for a long time. Parents respond
very differently to baby boys and girls. Both mothers and
fathers use many more terms of endearment when addressing
their baby girls. When parents were requested by researchers
to "Get their infant to smile and to vocalize," fathers and
mothers expended much more effort trying with their baby
girls. Since baby boys and baby girls do not differ in their
basic ability to smile or vocalize, inborn skills are not what
prompt differences in parents' participation.

The Creation of Imagination

Imitation begins to play an important role in your baby's
learning now. It is a wonderful way to learn. Even a baby
who has never before learned a piece of behavior by watching someone else will do so at this stage. Although still very
fragile, you can use imitation in your baby's *second year* to
institute toilet training, toothbrushing, and washing the hands
and face. Don't be tempted to push it too hard now because
you recognize its potential for learning. Mothers who *have*
pushed have found that their babies' imitation vanished.

Your baby usually will have no qualms about spontaneously
identifying with your behavior. He will try to feed you pieces
of food, as you have fed him. If you accept them, he is
thrilled, laughs when you smack your lips, and watches your
chewing and swallowing intently. He dabs at his face with a
washcloth in imitation of your washing, and laughs when you
imitate his posture and movements after him. When you take
your baby from the bathtub and say "brr" and shiver as you
dry him, the baby will laugh and try imitating you. As he
imitates, he learns some things about cold—the feeling of
being chilled, and the way people react to it physically and
vocally.

Believe it or not, he will begin picking up some of your
less stellar traits as well. If you are compulsively clean, he
may swipe away at his feeding table with a towel in imitation
of your cleaning gestures. He will spill very little as he brings

his spoon to his mouth, and zealously dab his mouth or the tray when he does. Sometimes this isn't good. Babies are naturally messy and precise neatness is unusual at this age. Some baby girls, more than baby boys, show this, but they really aren't old enough to understand the meaning of cleanliness as we do. If a child senses you are upset at his messiness, he may conclude that he must become antiseptically clean; he may get pretty compulsive himself, and very upset when he gets dirty. Then he may be afraid to explore the world freely the way a baby usually does to get acquainted with it.

A baby also imitates other babies. On some days in a doctor's office, a baby can initiate a chorus of crying or laughter by this imitative contagion. If you visit another family with a baby, yours may appear engrossed, though removed from their baby's activity. When you return home, you may see yours imitate the other's play as if he has learned it all. A precocious ten-month-old is perfectly capable of removing the rings from the tower color cone he never played with before and piling them back on their spindle exactly as he saw the other baby do it. Twins are especially fine mimics. Often one twin is the doer and the other watches. The "watcher" can suddenly perform in full a routine that this twin has spent days mastering.

Representational memory—memory of behavior and of things seen but out of sight—is the basis of imitation and something else related to it, which psychologists call "object permanence." The baby can retain events for longer and longer periods. He is just beginning to recognize that time is a medium in which he, as well as objects, can be located in relationship to each other.

Memory for what is out of sight grows together with understanding of distance and depth to help the baby imitate behavior and understand the nature of objects. Now he can reach behind himself for a toy as he sits, without turning to look at it, because he has learned that an unseen object has not necessarily disappeared, and he has discovered how to gauge the distance between himself and an object he wants, even with his eyes averted or closed. Not-so-near space isn't a single flat plane any more, either. The baby's eye and mind can perceive it ranged into regions of differing depths.

Many objects are now becoming detached and independent entities that can be imitated, inserted in play routines, and related in space, time, and cause-and-effect sequences. They can also be studied, and their qualities fully explored from all aspects. Give your baby something you do not mind being ruined and watch him closely. He will probably vary what he does to the object to see how his actions affect it. Instead of just paying attention to his act of letting go, he now heeds the motion of his cup as it splatters to the floor. You rush to clean up the mess. Meantime, the baby studiously looks at it and tries to pick it up if you will let him. A grownup's earliest memories may include a scene of himself as a toddler plopping an egg onto his grandmother's oriental rug, and the confusing hysteria of all the females in the household merely because he wanted to see what would happen to it when it fell.

A baby studies displacements very attentively, rolls a ball from the couch to the armchair, then back again; repeatedly stacks a series of rings on his stacking toy color cone; swipes his mother's jewelry box from her dresser, removes the bracelets, rings and earrings, then replaces them all as best he can; rotates and reverses his bottle and sets it by his plate on his feeding tray. He tries to accommodate features of unfamiliar objects instead of treating them as though they had all the properties of the nearest equivalent, familiar things.

He deliberately hides and finds his brother's coloring book under the scatter rug, and removes an obstacle to reach for the toy he can see or even one he cannot. The baby begins to learn that just because his toy truck is not around it has not vanished from the face of the earth. He discovers that the truck-on-the-couch and the truck-under-the-chair are the same, no matter where they are.

Now your baby can anticipate the return of a person or thing that he has released, manually or visually. You can tell because he is able to leave and return to you at will, allow you to leave him, and anticipate your return. If you ask your baby now to find a toy you have hidden, he will probably be able to find it if he has watched you hide it and you do not ask him to find it too long afterward. If he accidentally drops his toy behind an armchair, he might actually struggle to shove the chair away because he knows it's down there. His remembering, searching, and refusal to be diverted by other "finds" is the first step toward the more prolonged concentration of adults, and away from the distractibility characteristic of infancy and early childhood. In experiments at

Harvard's Center for Cognitive Studies, Mrs. Judith Gardner found that young infants do not try to search for an object that they have watched disappear behind a screen. Somewhat older ones will visually track over the path the object followed before it disappeared. Only babies in the last several months of their first year begin to search beyond the disappearance point.

A baby's accomplishments in this department are still young. For example, if his ball rolls under an armchair, he hefts the chair away from the wall to get it. Should it roll under the loveseat, which is too heavy for him to shove, he will give up after a few nudges, and crawl to the armchair where he was more successful! A bit later, he will be clever enough to search *only* where the object was last seen.

Without this beginning concept of "object permanence," the baby would be very uncomfortable about rolling (dropping would be more accurate) a ball to his brother to throw back to him. As the baby plays with his brother, he *foresees* return of the ball he has thrown and is disappointed if his brother fails him.

Most wonderful of all, as the baby grows in his ability to distinguish people and things from their surroundings, he begins to sense that he himself is a person and an object among others. His whole body, as well as parts of it such as his hands and feet, are in space. *He* has his own texture, resistance, locomotive style, and he exists in relationship to other objects and people in his world.

Motor

Large

Crawls on straightened limbs.

Stands with little support.
May get self to stand
independently by straightening
limbs and pushing up and off
from palms.
Side-steps along furniture.
Walks holding two hands.
Climbs up and down from chairs.

Sitting

Sits down from standing.
Gets onto stomach from sitting.

Small

Carries two small objects in one
hand.
Dangles object from string.

May differentiate use of hands,
holding with one, maneuvering
with other.

Releases grasped object
awkwardly.

Small muscle control of rectum.

Language

Active

Learns words and appropriate
gestures; e.g., says *No* and shakes
head; *Bye-bye* and waves.
May repeat word incessantly,
making it a response to every
question.
May say one or two words besides
Mama and *Dada*.

Passive

Listens with interest to familiar
words.
Understands and obeys words and
commands, e.g., *Give it to me*.

Please do not regard this chart as a rigid timetable. Babies are unpredictable. Some perform an activity earlier or later than the chart indicates.

Growth Chart

Mental

Reaches behind him for a toy without seeing it.
Ranges distant space into regions of differing depths.

Sees individual objects as separate from others. Continues to learn about properties of objects; crumples paper, rattles box, listens to watch tick.
Points, pokes, touches, and pries with extended index finger.
Looks for contents of box. Grasps small objects in container. Looks at pellet if it drops out of container.

Searches for hidden object if he sees it hidden. Lifts inverted box or cup in search of toy. Searches briefly for object in second hiding place; if unsuccessful, returns to first hiding place. Searches in same place for object he has seen hidden in various locations.

Increasingly imitates behaviors; rubs self with soap, feeds others.

Begins to sense he is an object among others.
Begins to prefer one hand and side of body to the other.
Points to body parts.

Tries out new acts for same goal, modifies old ones through trial and error.

Matches two blocks.

Social

Personal

Shows moods, looks hurt, sad, happy, uncomfortable, angry, and shows preferences, likes music.

Identifies body parts.
Imitates gestures, facial expressions, sounds.
Begins sexual identity, e.g., boys begin identifying with males; girls with females.
Grows aware of self, social approval and disapproval; interaction.

Interaction

More sensitive toward other children, cries if other child receives attention.

Fears performing familiar activities, may regress to earlier stages.

Pulls off hat for fun.
Prefers one or several toys; shows tenderness toward stuffed animal or doll.

Cultural

Helps hold cup for drinking. Feeds self whole meals.

May have trouble sleeping.

Helps dress self.

THE
ELEVENTH
MONTH
A Proper Person

THE ELEVENTH MONTH
A Proper Person

During this month your baby is most likely to stand alone. His control of his upright body will improve as he gets used to being on his feet. He is becoming quite a handy little fellow. But as in the previous month, much of his energy and attention is turned to "social improvement," despite his extra dependence on you. He makes extensive use of imitation, his learning technique for discovering what people are all about. He grows more and more aware of approval and disapproval. Since being refused and limited, even "for your own good," is often hard for a baby to take, this can be a difficult time, especially when he is so engrossed in his preparations for walking.

Standing may become so important that your baby refuses to lie down. He stands next to furniture, he stands in the middle of the floor, he stands in his feeding chair, in his bath, as he is changed. He falls asleep standing in his crib. He stands for his examination by his pediatrician. Standing, he "helps" with his dressing. Holding onto your shoulders as you put on his overalls, he lifts one leg and then the other. Obediently he raises his arms so you can pull off his undershirt. Anything, as long as he is on his feet.

He becomes a public menace in his stroller. On the way to the grocery store, he stands and cranes over to snatch at passersby or claw at objects on the ground. Once inside, he stands and stretches for a large can of tomato sauce or a tantalizing bunch of grapes. Unless you constantly watch him, he is bound to fall. If you decide to find a harness for him, get one that gives him the freedom to stand and lean over, but prevents his tumbling out. But even if your baby is wearing a harness, he can pull his stroller over on top of himself unless it is solidly built.

His experimenting with standing may lead to other skills. As he topples forward, the momentum teaches him a new way to crawl. Arms and legs straightened out, bottom wagging left and right, he crawls on his "stilts" across the room. Climbing stairs is the next step, although coming down may not be so easy. You may find yours part way up the stairs, pivoting around and ready to rocket into space, or perched precariously at the top of the staircase, on the verge of toppling down. Putting gates across the stairs will stop him for a while. One day, however, he may find the gate open and try to climb. Although a stair carpet will cushion a fall, the best safeguard in the long run is to try and teach your baby to climb in both directions. Although he may seem glued to his forward direction at first and unwilling or unable to try reverse, your persistence should pay off in his eventual understanding.

The baby may add other maneuvers to his standing ability, including squatting and stooping. Just as he did when sitting, he will deliberately lean over and pick up a toy he has dropped. He squats, scoops the toy up in one hand, stands, then squats, and scoops with the other. He is playing with the sensation of doing the same thing with different sides of his body. Then he stoops to collect his toy with *either* hand while he anchors himself with the free one at an armchair. These variations show the baby's increasing interest in depth and distance and his curiosity about how different maneuvers, such as dropping, will affect an object. Will it split, shatter, bounce, or clink when it hits? They also show his improving control of his body against gravity and illustrate his ability to use both hands simultaneously for different activities. The baby can hold a toy in one hand while pulling to stand with the other.

Your baby's manipulative behavior may be quite agile. Single-handedly he can carry his spoon to his mouth once you fill it for him. With both hands, he can hold his cup. Using one hand for picking up and eating bits of food and the other for complex maneuvers with the spoon is still a bit difficult. If he can pull off his socks and shirt, pull out shoelaces, and untie his own when asked, he is doing very well indeed.

If your baby seems anxious to walk, you may consider getting a walker for him. Before you do, try to imagine its potential effect on him—particularly if he is highstrung. Some babies react almost hysterically to the precocious mastery of a step and become too dependent on anything that helps with it. Dr. Brazelton writes about a baby boy who as soon as he was placed in a walker became a little wild man, "losing contact with everything around him, propelling himself forward to the right, to the left, into furniture, bouncing over thresholds from one room to the other. No one could reach him, and he could not stop moving. When he was finally taken out, he screamed wildly as if separated from something desperately important to him." When he is ready, a baby commits all his pent-up energy to learning to walk. When he no longer has to learn for himself because he has a crutch, his own efforts may be checked and his unused energy makes him a very tense and unhappy person.

A baby enjoys his own experimentation much more. Some even discover their own crutch to walk with, often making themselves walkers from small chairs. Your baby, in leaning against a small chair, may make it move unexpectedly. Quite able to associate cause with effect now, he realizes that he has caused its motion. He pushes again and it slides again. If your baby happens to have selected your favorite Chippendale, turn another small chair on its back and let your baby practice with it. He may spend a fair portion of his day pushing and staggering along behind it. Besides being fun, this is a real teaching device. A baby gets the basic idea of walking by feeling and watching his weight shifting from foot to foot as he picks up each foot. Apparently babies have enjoyed this game for a long time. Many old wooden chairs are flattened on the backs of the posts from some baby's pushing on hard floors long ago.

Since babies are individuals, all eleven-month-olds do not perform the same miracles. Many are still not standing alone, while others are already walking by themselves. A very precocious baby will actually prefer to walk than crawl now. In contrast, a quiet baby is just standing supported. He may let his parents put him in a standing position, but he is clearly most excited when he laboriously hauls himself up. Unlike more active learners, he is slower, but often more sure. He never tumbles backward from his new height, and when he comprehends the technique, he lets himself down gradually to sitting. Once he has mastered that hurdle, he feels less anxious about playing on his feet. If this sounds more like your baby, do not worry if some toddlers in the neighborhood seem more adept. Your baby's progress is average, not delayed. According to developmental norms based on studies of thousands of youngsters, the average age range for walking alone in the United States is twelve to fourteen months.

In addition, many quiet infants have a "flop-jointed" body type. They have rubbery, over-extensible joints that easily bend beyond a natural extended position and hardly seem to anchor anywhere at all. This kind of jointing makes loco-motion harder, even when a baby wants to move. To give firmness to his joints when he stands and walks, the baby's musculature must be developed more than usual. So the child has to practice longer to gain the extra muscular strength he needs. Perhaps the quiet temperament that often accompanies the flop-jointed body type appropriately deters the inner-directed surge of physical activity until the body is able to handle it.

Many mothers are concerned because their infants, when they start to stand, seem to have "rolled-in" or pronated feet. They balance with their legs apart on the inner edges of their feet and ankles rather than on the soles. As the baby's bal-ance improves, he will no longer need this wide base of sup-port. His feet and arches will strengthen and he will start "toeing in."

Some infants, however, toe in so much at the beginning that they occasionally stumble over their own feet. These babies should be left barefooted or given soft, flexible shoes, which are better for their feet and let their toes grip the ground. If your baby continues to have trouble, consult your pediatrician before he gets a bad feeling about walking. After your baby has walked about a month, your pediatrician should evaluate his feet and legs anyway.

The right shoes are especially important now. Dr. Brazelton indicates that "slick, hard-soled shoes, which many old-school sitters and grandmothers think necessary for 'foot support,' slip." Shoes must fit perfectly and should not be too big to "allow for growth." Large shoes increase tripping and accentuate the way a baby walks, throwing his feet in or out to avoid the extra toe space.

More on Imitation

The imitation of the previous month is even more marked now. One of the basic requirements for the baby's imitative flair is the ability to remember behavior so that he can reproduce it. The baby must also have the ability to associate behavior and qualities with people and things. If your baby points upward when you say "airplane" or tries to meow when you show him a kitten, he is beginning to correctly associate certain qualities with their objects.

He will also play with differences. Dropping one object

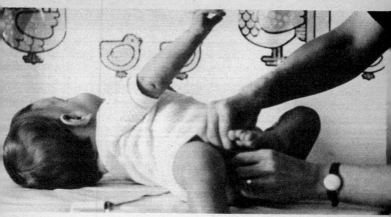

after another into a cup, he seems to hear the difference in the clunk of a block and the ring of a metal ball. If he tries the same thing with a glass, he will notice the new sounds the block and ball create against this new substance. When he tries to retrieve the objects from the glass, he first tries to reach them through its sides. Then he reaches into the open end. Although he has poured objects from a cup before, he has to relearn with a glass container because the visual cues from its transparent sides confuse him despite the familiar shapes and behavior. At first confounded because the total situation is different, the baby eventually breaks the whole scene into its component bits, learns to associate the containers despite their different materials, and later generalizes his new information about glass to other glass things.

A mirror is a bit trickier. Although he has learned to differentiate the mirror images of himself and his parents from reality, he may still reach for the reflection of a favorite toy. He may catch his mistake when he knocks his hand against the mirror.

Despite minor imperfections in technique, imitation proves more and more deliberate, sophisticated, and useful to the baby. He can cleverly reverse and adopt behavior he has watched. For example, your baby may hide a favorite toy of his brother's or sister's and laugh merrily when they find it. Since they have taught him the game with his toys and laughed at his discovery, he is a bit misled by their lack of amusement.

Through imitating, the baby also learns to talk and dress himself. From observing you dress him, he begins to help wiggle into clothes, pull off shirts when asked, stick his foot into a shoe, and figure out which leg or arm to extend. He tries to pull off his socks by catching the toe and pulling. But so far, he pulls backward and has little success unless the sock is practically off his foot anyway.

In learning to talk, a baby will copy his parents' inflections, as well as speech rhythms, and even produce facial attitudes in comically close mimicry. Your baby will try to approximate speech sounds, too. Though certain words are clearly familiar to him because he babbles back more when he hears them, his production of them lags behind his understanding. A few, mumbled sequences may sound like *mama, dada, bye-bye, no-no,* but most of his speech is still gibberish.

During his prewalking stage, with all its exciting but frightening freedom, the baby is still very dependent on you. He

identifies closely with your behavior and tries to imitate you at every turn. You may find him a constant attendant as he follows you about all day. If you wear a scarf on your hair as you work, he finds an old scarf to put on or wears the dust rag on his head. He begins to wipe the counter when you do, stir clumsily with a spoon as you are whipping up a cake, hang on heavily to the vacuum cleaner when you try to clean. He "goes and gets" simple objects for you and seems delighted when he returns with something you have asked for. He may even stand between your legs, leaning on them whenever you stop long enough, so that you have to step over him and may even trip on him during the day.

He watches you rock in a chair, crawls up into it, pushes you to get out, and begins to rock himself. He closes his eyes and hums just like mother when she is content. Although you probably rocked your baby when he was smaller, it now becomes novel, because the baby can do it for himself.

The baby's dependence on you is balanced by his increasing independence with his sibs and his attraction to his father. The baby will imitate the way his sibs play with toys, whack the floor with a toy hammer in delight, and jab at paper with a crayon as his sibs color. When his brother takes his hand to show him how to crayon, he pulls away and refuses to be shown. Even though he rejects the demonstration, his next efforts are closer to the scribbling motions his brother has tried to show him.

Almost all babies at this age are attached to their fathers and anticipate his homecoming at day's end. They act as if he behaves differently toward them and they are right. Fathers smile and talk less than mothers, but they are more interested in getting their babies actively involved in their physical environment. A baby boy especially enjoys "roughhousing" with father. Being bounced on daddy's foot, or thrown in the air, or picked up and spun around, jouncing on his back, or crawling all over him are great fun. The more violent the play, the better the baby likes it, as you can tell by his protests when your husband finally decides he wants to eat his dinner or read the newspaper. Some mothers see this turning to father as the baby's fatigue at being isolated with a female all day and as a desire for novelty. While this is partly true for all babies, your husband gives your baby boy an extension of his own active development, plus the chance to identify with another male. Just as a little girl is beginning to sense her femininity, the baby boy begins to realize some of his masculine identity.

No, No, a Thousand Times No

A baby this age is quite devoted to finding out about himself. As he stands and stoops, he is not just practicing physical skills. He is comparing the feeling of doing something with different sides of his body to see if there are various ways to achieve the same thing.

Another important part of a baby's identity is his ability to establish the meaning of "No." Like standing, he must experiment with and practice it day and night. He will shake his head and say "No" to everything—even when he means "Yes." He loves the head movement and times his "No" so that it fits each swing. He is so taken with it, he may spend a whole meal flinging his head and refusing to eat. He refuses to cooperate during his bath—and catching his face to wash it as he swings his head is a real trick. He shakes his head through diaper changes and waggles his body in a total negative.

Along with a baby's ability to say "No" comes the realization of what the "No" of others means. Your baby will grow more aware of the difference between being good and being naughty. When he is "good," he constantly seeks your approval; for example, after he pulls on his sock or makes a block tower of two blocks, he calls out "See," with a grin that requests an approving comment. After he dutifully eats some of his lunch, he holds up the dish to be admired. When he finishes his bottle, he holds it out—shaking it to show how empty it is. When he finishes his evening bottle in the dark, he wants you to turn on the light and admire its transparency before he allows you to put him to sleep.

He is also conscious of the implications of his naughtiness. He learns to turn on the television. Frightened when it comes on with a blast, he scrambles to another room and waits for someone to turn down the volume. He learns rapidly that the sudden blare will bring someone. He has to be reminded repeatedly to leave it alone. Before he flushes the toilet in the bathroom, he pauses to look around hastily, then pulls the handle anyway. When his father comes to check his antics, he stands behind the bathroom door half-hidden and completely abashed.

When he is about to get into trouble, he looks at you as if to say, "Don't come after me," then scurries to his brother's toy chest (definitely off-limits), glances over his shoulder to check, lifts the lid, snatches a toy, and unwittingly lets the lid slam. He tucks the toy under his arm to conceal it, then crawls to a safe spot to enjoy himself. If you catch him at his play, his eyes widen, and he smiles foolishly.

Clearly the baby knows what he is doing. He understands the meaning of "No" and some implications of his behavior. As early as seven months of age, a baby can appear sheepish about being caught at something he is not supposed to do. Now he is a bit more aware of simple cause-and-effect actions. His repetition of your favorite swear word is breathlessly expectant because he is already aware of its specialness in *your* repertoire. You may find your baby's hearing ability gauged to his motivation and interest in performing what you request. Poor hearing can accompany things he does not want to hear, while he listens raptly to the ticking of his father's watch or your whispered "Want a cookie?" from across the room.

He is also becoming increasingly handy and mobile. Since he can move far and fast enough from you in a suddenly bigger and not always safe world, you must begin to set limits on his travels. Luckily, a baby's obedience and attachments to specific people develop at about the same time as his locomotion and comprehension of simple utterances. A baby at this age can understand his own "No" and simple commands so he can heed and comply with his mother's "No-no" and simple prohibitions. He is also able to understand more complicated demands, not necessarily because he comprehends the words being used, but because you amply cue him to your wishes by your facial expressions, tone of voice, and gestures. Some babies can also comply with known commands by stopping their own approach to a previously tabooed area or their reach for a forbidden object, mumbling "No-no" all the while or wagging their heads assertively as if to reinforce their own conviction. Such early self-control, by the way, has been experimentally associated with intelligence.

About the same time, your baby will try to test your "No." When you are near, he may spend most of his time teasing you, pulling at your skirt, yanking at your shoes, banging your book. When you try to ignore him, he deliberately gets himself into spots where he needs help or goes for a "no," such as an electric outlet, the TV, or the stove. If you do not object immediately, he may slow his pace and turn. When he sees you are watching, he smiles and continues full steam ahead. Usually, he is not even interested in the forbidden object per se because he rarely returns to it unless he has your attention. Often a child will try this game even when he has understood the rationale for the "No" and has accepted the prohibition.

Sometimes his testing is even more disturbing. At night, after he is in his crib, he will call you as many times as you will come. You or his father will have to be firm or he will grow more and more demanding as the atmosphere tightens to the breaking point. Though still early, a few eleven-month-olds may begin consciously using tantrums as they recognize their power to control people in their world. When your baby wants a cookie that does not appear or a brother's toy that is off-limits, you may be stunned to see him drop dramatically to the floor, screeching and kicking in protest. Surprised and a bit overcome at his new "temper," you may at first give in rather than watch him scream. *Once is enough.* With that kind of encouragement, the baby will plummet into his routine every time he is refused something. Babies are quite clever about figuring out the appropriate behavior for the right person. If his regular sitter is singularly unimpressed, he will save his performance just for you.

Rather than punishing and confusing your baby, try to let him collapse and scream on the floor without responding. He will probably kick louder and roll his head even more at first. But if you persist long enough, he will probably quiet eventually—maybe with even a glance of surprise at you—and wordlessly resume his play. A calm end to such an episode is your sign that your baby is not in any real trouble. When a toddler has a real temper tantrum, he just cannot turn it off so easily.

The basic curbs to a baby's naughtiness are the same, though they may come from other family members too. Since you are not always speedy enough in removing the baby, an older child may learn to handle his "No's" himself. A sister's anger when the baby pulls over her doll table full of china may stop retrials permanently. Rather than anger, judiciously ignoring the baby's antics sometimes works. Often diversion is the answer. For example, when your eldest son drags the baby away from his toy chest by the legs, he only triggers another game. He pulls and baby waits until dumped across the room. Then he scrambles back. After all, brother means fun so far. But "No," and enticing the baby away with another toy works. Brother calls from another room or drags a toy before the baby's following nose, then quickly jumps to slam the lid on the toy chest. Your three-year-old learns what it takes many mothers months to discover. Simply removing a baby from a goal without a change of interest only challenges him to repeat his original investigations more vigorously.

Sometimes you just have to say "No" forcefully. The baby may startle, turn to look at you to see if you mean it, pucker as if to cry, then finally pivot and go to something else. Although a few babies appear to know enough to stop themselves, most can get carried away and push their testing too far. Allowing anything as dangerous as a stove to be used to tease and involve you is foolish.

An experienced mother can be comfortable in a disciplinary role and not worry that the baby's feelings may be hurt by her sudden sharpness. A new mother and father, on the other hand, can feel very guilty when their baby looks wounded after they have taken a stand, although this does not negate its importance.

The best way to insure a willingness to comply is not extensive training, discipline, or other massive attempts to modify the infant's natural course of development. It is a healthy, harmonious relationship between mother and baby. You can misuse the baby's attachment to you by curtailing his necessary explorations or you can use it positively, permitting him the freedom to grow and learn and limiting him only when he is in danger, or when you must for the sake of others in the family.

In a fascinating study, Dr. Mary D. Ainsworth of The Johns Hopkins University found that mother's discipline—the frequency of her commands and physical interventions—did not improve the baby's compliance with her commands. Quite the contrary, the more floor freedom she gave the baby, the more likely the baby was to control his own behavior. She found that certain motherly qualities—sensitivity to, acceptance of, and cooperation with the baby—were especially associated with the baby's obedience. Dr. Ainsworth says,

"The sensitive mother is aware of, accurately interprets and responds promptly and appropriately to the baby's signals and communications, and is able to see things from his point of view. The insensitive mother is geared almost exclusively to her own wishes, moods, and activity. Her interventions tend to be prompted by her own signals and so rarely relate to the baby's.

"The accepting mother accepts almost all aspects of the baby's behavior, including those things other mothers find hurtful or distasteful, and she also accepts the responsibility of caring for him without chafing at the temporary restriction of her usual activities. The rejecting mother may feel positively about her baby but is frequently overwhelmed by resentment and anger—which she may voice openly or display less overtly in her behavior toward him and her comments about him. The co-operative mother avoids imposing her will on the baby, and arranges the environment and her schedule to minimize any need to interrupt or to control him. When she intervenes she is adept at 'mood setting' which helps him to accept her wishes or controls as something congenial to him. At the other extreme, the interfering mother does not consider her baby as a separate person whose activities and wishes have a validity of their own. She seems to assume that she has a perfect right to do with him what she wishes, imposing her will on his, shaping him to her standards, and interrupting him arbitrarily without regard for his moods, wishes, or activity-in-progress."

Those mothers judged to be sensitive, accepting of the baby, and co-operative by these standards had babies who were naturally and willingly compliant to their commands. As Dr. Ainsworth points out, "The first and most important step in socializing a human being is a baby's willingness to do as he is asked. So the growth of an initial, unspecific disposition toward compliance may be critical for all later social development and learning."

Motor

Large

Stands alone.
Gets self to stand by straightening limbs and pushing up and off from palms, lifting trunk.
May get self to stand by flexing knees, pushing off from squat.
May stand alone and wave.
May stand against support and lean over.
Standing, may pivot body 90 degrees.
Walks holding one or two hands.
Climbs up stairs.

Sitting

Squats and stoops.

Small

Holds crayons, makes marks.
Grasps bell handle.

May carry spoon to mouth.

May use hands in sequence, e.g., in feeding, or simultaneously, e.g., squats, picks up object in one hand, holds onto support with other.

May pull off socks, untie shoe-laces.

Language

Active

Speech still primarily gibberish with a few intelligible sounds.

Imitates inflections, speech rhythms, facial attitudes more accurately than speech sounds.

Says two or three words besides *Mama, Dada*.
Mumbles word or words for long periods.

May use jargon, sentences of gibberish in which meaningful words are sometimes embedded.
May express thoughts with single word.

Passive

Begins to differentiate between words.

Recognizes words as symbols for objects: airplane, points to sky; doggie, growls.

Please do not regard this chart as a rigid timetable. Babies are unpredictable. Some perform an activity earlier or later than the chart indicates.

Growth Chart

Mental

Points at object through glass.
May try to grab it through side of
glass.
Explores container-contained
relationship. Fingers holes in a
form board. Lifts lid from box.
Unwraps cube. Pokes clapper of
bell.
Places and removes objects such
as a small block or spool into
and from cup or box.

Increases imitation. Imitates
scribble, ringing of bell.

Aware of his own actions and
some of their implications.
Compares same act done with
each side of the body. May use
both hands simultaneously for
different functions.

Experiments with means to attain
goal; e.g., uses small chair as a
walker.

Associates properties with things:
meows for kitten, points upward
when he sees bird.

May remove and place rings on a
tower cone. May nest series of
boxes. Turns pages of a book, not
necessarily one at a time.

Looks at pictures in book with
interest.

Social

Personal

Reaches for mirror images of
objects.

Asserts self among sibs.

Interaction

Increases dependence on mother.
May infer some of mother's
goals and her plans to achieve
them. Begins trying to alter them
through persuasion or protest.

Obeys commands. May inhibit
his own behavior.
Seeks approval. Tries to avoid
disapproval.

Is not always cooperative. Refuses
forceful teaching; opposes
removal of toys; extends but
does not release toy to person;
likes imitating, then doing for
himself; protests curtailment of
play.
Establishes meaning of "No."
Shows guilt at wrongdoing.
May tease and test parental limits.

Imitates movements of adults
and movements and play of other
children.
Plays parallels to, not with,
another child.

THE TWELFTH MONTH

Stepping Out

THE TWELFTH MONTH
Stepping Out

By the twelfth month, many babies are ready to walk. This fascinating activity distracts the baby from what his mother and most adults consider basics—eating and sleeping. But there are even more profound consequences. The baby is able to get to people and things and to explore space and objects by himself in a way that will be far more efficient than crawling. He is also more independent of adult control. Yet fearful of this independence, he again grows anxious about strangers and separations from you. Beyond this, the balance between freedom and containment becomes an issue that you and your baby must mutually solve.

Walking is the crowning achievement of this long and exciting "motor" year. The stepping reflex the baby had during his first week of life and even more noticeably toward the end of his first month may have allowed your baby to take as many as fifteen consecutive steps across the floor as you held him gently under the arms. For a long time this reflex disappeared, only to surface again right after the middle of the year as the baby voluntarily stamped one foot or the other and pumped his whole body up and down as you held him under the arms. Later when you held him by the hands, he deliberately stepped in place and finally he took his first steps with you. (Many babies are still at that point this month or are just managing to stand alone.)

The first unsupported steps are often accidental. Perhaps you let go of his hands as you are walking him and before he quite realizes it, he has taken a step unassisted. Then frustrated at being deserted, he flops to the floor. Sometimes it happens as a baby practices his standing maneuvers. Just as he did when was perfecting his sitting skill, he twists the upper part of his body to reach for a toy behind him or to wave at you. At first he holds onto a prop to steady himself. Then he tries it without support. Soon he learns to balance as he turns by holding out *his* arms. Next, he pivots his *whole* body in sections—first the upper half, then the lower —by lurching around with arms carefully extended for balance. Believe it or not, these are the first unsupported steps.

Soon he applies the balance he has gained from turning. He spreads his wings, spinning his forearms and hands in tight flat circles for a kind of rotating propulsion. Straining every muscle, he begins to take steps from one to the other of you. He glues his eyes on his target, face drawn and intent, and totters forward on his toes. Squealing with joy, he collapses during his remaining steps toward waiting arms.

Within a week, he can navigate the expanse of an entire room. Arms high, with stiffened knees and a wide-legged gait, he swings his body sideways with each leg thrust. Like a bandy-legged old sailor, he clumps across the floor, sometimes losing his footing on the hardwood floor or a scatter rug. Cheerful about his downfalls, he simply gets himself together, pushes back to stand, and unless he stumbles again in the same spot, exuberantly shoves off again.

He learns how to slow down, catch himself, and turn around, and soon steers around edges and corners. Last of all, he learns to stop himself. Stopping in the middle of the floor is a real achievement. First stops are effected by falling or by clutching at passing people or furniture. When he finally can halt at will, he practices it constantly.

In a matter of a week, he changes from a person who looks as if he wants to but does not dare to one who cannot get enough. Parental praise and enthusiasm can noticeably lengthen the stretches of steps he takes before tripping. With or without you, he staggers, topples, halts, but always starts forward again hour after hour. You may be fascinated with your baby's tireless, almost feverish devotion. The exuberance and accomplishment radiating from your baby's face show his recognition that he has attained another major goal. Babies are so consumed by their own walking prowess that they will actually swagger off the top of a table from which they have cautiously crawled only a few months before.

His determination when he first walks affords a precious glimpse of the inner force that pushes young animals from one level of development to the next and drives them to conquer their environments. His feelings also testify to the joy and pride that come from doing something by oneself.

Walking will be an unwieldy accomplishment for a long

time. It definitely should not be considered a performance
for others, particularly people the baby considers strangers,
in a strange place. It still demands the infant's total concentration. Crawling is baby's business approach to his
environment, the one he uses when he really wants to go
places fast or freely explore strange scenery. Just as you
could tell around the half-year mark how new the baby's sitting skill was by the height of his arms, you can gauge his
prowess in walking by whether or not he needs to extend
his arms high. As his walking balance improves, he will
gradually lower his arms. This important step means that a
baby has learned to balance himself from within his body, by
controlling the muscles of his trunk. Then he can master
other maneuvers, such as using his hands while he walks.
The first such actions are usually in rhythm with the legs'
motion because they can be assimilated better into the
total body action. Partly for this reason, partly because it is
so social, one of the first additions to walking is waving and
saying "bye-bye." The baby learns to flap his hand as you
leave the room.

Those babies who have been walking for a couple of
months may be adding more complicated maneuvers. Yours
may balance his toys as he walks. Much like an older child
walking on a fence, he holds his full hands high. Or he may
walk backward, pulling a toy so he can watch it as he pulls
(even though he backs right into furniture). Walking backward is easier for your baby than you might guess—creeping
and crawling, after all, began backward.

For most babies, walking is a rather rigid task. The baby
is not at ease enough yet to take pieces of the whole performance and translate them readily to other physical skills.
Pushing himself in a kiddy car, for example, which also
requires alternating use of the legs, takes many weeks to
learn. He may inch along tagging after a brother and sister
on their tricycles. First he will push with both feet, sometimes
with one at a time, then both again laboriously. Alternating
the feet to push is just different enough from alternating
them to walk to cause difficulty. The baby has to balance
seated instead of upright and he must also push back against
the ground, as well as down. Recognizing the rigidity with
which infants learn many skills, Dr. Myrtle McGraw, former
director of developmental psychology at Briarcliff College and
a leader in infant research for almost four decades, has

actually taught rollerskating to babies. She trains them *after* they have learned to balance upright, but *before* they have locked into a specific way to displace their body weight forward.

Walking has a curious companion. Just as it appears, swimming behavior begins to show in the tub. Like walking, swimming goes through three phases. Newborns have a reflex ability to swim. They can squiggle through the water quite competently. Then for a long stretch after their third month, they have trouble in the water. Now if you support your baby gently under the chest, his body will undulate, his arms will circle naturally at his sides, and his legs will kick alternately. These swimming movements are inherited from our amphibious ancestors. Infants are naturally beguiled by water and love swimming. They will swagger in over their heads unless carefully watched. Fear of water and of getting one's head under the surface comes in the second or third year because of greater awareness of what water can do. Before this fear develops, teaching an infant to swim is quite easy. Unless swimming is continued regularly from this time on, however, these movements will be abandoned as sensory experience and judgment expand.

Handy Man

Walking, the most visible and dramatic physical achievement, tends to mask other exciting physical happenings of this period in your baby's life. As you may have noticed to your amusement and dismay, your baby is becoming more and more handy even though he still cannot handle many things well. Try to offer him a bowl and watch his "overlap grasp" as he takes it from you. Until he is about eighteen months old, he will place his fingers on the inside of the bowl, his thumb on the outside, and the rim in the palm.

Still, he has come a long way. One reason is that some of the bones of his hand and wrist are now firm. Instead of the soft cartilage of early infancy, the baby has more to work with. From the visibly labored eye-hand coordination he achieved in grasping at six months, he can now reach for something while looking the other way. From crude, raking motions with a clawlike hand, he comes to handle small items neatly with thumb and forefinger. From total involvement of his whole body, he has refined and limited his efforts to his arm and hand muscles. From the two-handed reach of midyear, he now offers a preferred hand along the line of sight.

Your baby, like most his age, is probably using the right hand as the active explorer and the left as a container and holder. At about four and one-half months of age, many infants use both hands equally. Now about 70 percent of them will accept a proffered object with the right hand. You will also see this preference in finger feeding, in reaching, and in thumb sucking. At Harvard's Center for Cognitive Studies, visiting infants show their end-of-year dexterity by pushing up and holding a sliding, see-through trap door with one hand and reaching inside for a toy with the other. A more precocious baby can rest his chin on his left hand while leaning on his left elbow and maneuver his push toys with his right hand.

Some babies now can hold onto more than a couple of things at a time. As you may recall, your baby at about seven months dropped a toy he was holding to take your offering—as long as you caught him before his toy was on its way to his mouth. Possibly at about ten months, he took the second toy in his free hand without dropping the first. If you offered a third plaything, one of the others had to go as he took the new one. Now if you offer him that third toy, he may put one of the first two in the crook of the opposite arm and take the new object with his free hand. As long as his arm holds out, he will continue to accept toys. He is becoming a competent tool user, just like other humans and very unlike most animals. By using his arms and hands as holders and movers, he is converting features of his world into means of attaining goals of his own choosing—in this instance, getting toys without using mother to do it for him. With this new confidence in his hands, he will become more and more free to use them for truly new methods of getting things done just for the fun of it.

With all these skills, some active twelve-month-olds can undress themselves completely whether you want them to or not. Your baby may untie his shoelaces, slip off his shoes and socks, or go the whole route, slip off overalls and diapers, and lurch out of the house. Reversing the overalls so the zipper or buttons are in back will avert this minor "disaster." One morning you may find your baby naked in bed, his clothes cast overboard. Perhaps because of your initial rewarding reaction, he may take off as many clothes as he can manage every nap and night. When he has had a bowel movement, the crib, of course, is a wreck. Sleepers with snappers in the back that are pinned securely or a sleeping bag with the zipper in the back will block his agile little hands.

Food? Forget It!

As you have probably learned over the past year, a major step such as walking has far-reaching implications for you. The baby's fervor and single-minded dedication to walking will interfere with his eating and sleeping. His awareness that walking is another means of bringing about separation from you will bring on a temporary period of fearfulness.

All this activity means the slowing of your baby's weight gain, even if he remains a good eater and enjoys every mouthful. Weight gain first slackens off for most babies by seven months, when they are crawling and losing interest in food. Now even more calories are burned as fuel for the baby's constant activity. Possibly his body is able to use less of what he eats because finger foods are not as thoroughly chewed and digested as mashed baby foods. Even so, your baby can absorb what he needs from a lumpy diet. The slowing of weight gain is good despite the once-popular belief that healthy babies are fat babies. At this stage your baby should be developing muscle tissue, not fat.

The independence that walking inspires may further complicate meals and vex mothers. In fact, the baby may begin to use food against you, much like his new "No's" and even tantrums, as one aspect of his self-differentiating and assertion over his environment. So forget your dreams of a three-meal-a-day, well-balanced diet for your baby. Do not be surprised if he eats one good meal, one so-so meal, and rejects another. He may have very definite likes and dislikes, refuse to try new foods, stick to only three or four favorites, and insist on feeding himself. You may lament all this, but trying to convert him to a well-rounded diet would be more trouble than it is worth. One good meal and four "acceptable" foods are par for the course for babies this age. Babies who comply with their mothers' notions of "a proper diet" are rarities. You will do a good job just sticking to the basic food requirements.

If you are still worried that the baby's new idiosyncracies will mean lower intake of essential foods, some pediatricians suggest waiting to wean him to the cup. Keeping the baby on the bottle allows him to meet his daily milk requirement of one pint since it provides a known quantity of milk. Having two ways to give him milk is also an asset if he is still unpredictable about using a cup. To cover some of his daily iron and most of his protein requirements, try adding an egg to his bottle when he refuses meat. If a bottle interferes with his appetite because his anticipation of it at a meal's end distracts him from solids, cut him down to two bottles of eight ounces each, and give them long enough after meals so the baby disassociates them. Knowing his needs are satisfied will allow you to relax and not push your baby to eat. Without pressure from you, he should not be a feeding problem by age three or so.

In fact, you should no longer be participating in his feedings at all. Many babies at this age interpret motherly participation as pressure and use it to key off a negative reaction to the whole meal. You might consider serving finger foods and leave choices to the child. In a now-famous experiment by Dr. Clara Davis, one-year-old babies who were allowed to choose freely from a buffet of wholesome foods, with no adult pressure, selected and ate what they required and rounded out their own diets over a month's time.

Some babies, however, still want an intimate give-and-take with mother. As long as your baby wants to be fed, feed him. Even babies who can hold their bottles and wield their own cups perfectly well may refuse to do so. Your baby may willingly accept utensils as playthings at mealtime and drink from a cup when you hold it for him, but wag his head emphatically and clench his hands when you try to place them around it—almost as if he feels that feeding him is still your job, which he is not going to assume. He may sense that as soon as he holds his own bottle and manipulates his cup or spoon he can be left alone with them, and he still prefers having you at hand.

Sleep? What's That?

Walking and the discoveries it allows may also mean increased resistance to bedtime. The baby cannot quite down when he is supposed to sleep and he wakes easily. For many babies, rocking on hands and knees and rolling and banging their heads, like thumbsucking, accompany gushes of physical growth. The leftover energy from the day's adventures must be expended in some way, either when the baby tries to sleep or wakes up to semiconsciousness. Rocking on his hands and knees, your baby may soon learn he can jounce his crib across the room to the wall, squeaking and banging against it alternately. Before he becomes used to the noises, it might be well to grease and tighten the screws of his crib.

Unless upsetting to other family members, these outlets should not be restricted. Thick rugs or rubber casters under the crib posts will help stop the sound carrying. Harnesses or other restraints, on the other hand, counteract the infant's natural urge to move and may make him hit his head more violently. The best way to help the baby is an after-dark session of crooning and gentle rocking as you feed him his last bottle. Although it may take as much as half an hour from your evening, feeling his tense little body begin to relax will be worth the time. Not only do you help the baby directly, you also set a valuable pattern for the future that he may include in his own repertoire. Being able to break from intense activity to relaxation is a must for many hardworking, driving adults.

The baby may also have trouble napping. After they learn to walk, babies are ready for one nap that fits into a daily pattern harmonious with the schedule of the rest of the family. Different infants have different cycles in this respect. But some babies, strange as it seems, are ready to nap in the morning soon after the night's long sleep. A morning nap, however, tends to make a baby fussy by midafternoon and too tired to eat his supper. A short collapse about 5:00 P.M. only refuels him for a long evening, and bedtime gets later and later. If your baby prefers a morning nap, you might begin delaying it until 11:00 A.M., then feed him a small lunch and put him down for two hours. When he wakes, feed him a second lunch, which will tide him over to an early supper. When he can last, feed him later, and gradually introduce him to a noon lunch and an early afternoon nap. This slow, steady pressure, an excellent way to adjust a baby's day, frees the evening for a needed respite from the baby, much as you love him.

Fearful Again

Coincident with rapidly increasing locomotion is a third phase of dependence on mother and fear of strange people and situations. The first usually occurs at four or five months with the thrust of visual development and the second at around eight months, when the baby can get about on the ground. Through with the frustration and emotional buildup before walking, the baby senses some of the consequences of being mobile. Just as he would insist on your pulling him up when he was learning to stand, now he will only walk holding onto your hands, and will totter only toward the arms of the people he trusts the most. He rightly distrusts his unpredictable sister, who is too easily diverted by any toy in her vicinity to catch him if he should topple. He may cling to you often, scamper after you when you leave a room, plead to be picked up, fuss in the evenings until you cuddle him, cry easily, and curl up in your arms when a new friend visits.

Many toddlers this age will still socialize with strangers in their own homes. Your baby may display his interest in socializing by fiercely hugging visiting toddlers, pressing them down when they try to stand, showing off his toys, and even permitting them to play with a few. But in the park, or yard, or during visits, he may clasp you tightly and refuse to join other youngsters.

Because of this intensified dependency, any separation from you, such as moving, hospitalization, or your long-awaited vacation will be particularly hard on your baby. If you must leave him, choose a caretaker such as a grandparent whom he knows and who knows him, who understands and accommodates to his ways. If he has a brother or sister, leave the sibling with the baby for comfort and company. In his own home, with his own routines, the loss will be easier for him to bear and the baby will cope with the new situation a little better. Caring for him will be easier, too.

While you are away, the baby may regress to an earlier stage of behavior. Many babies do this when they need to apply their energies to emotional adjustment. He may stop walking altogether, and his general progress may slacken, or he may be almost "too good." Even though he appears to have done well with familiar grandparents or a pleasant nurse, you should expect a reaction either immediately or soon after you return. You may find a very sober or a very aggressive baby. Once secure, he may kick the nurse about whom he could not dare reveal any bad feelings when he had only her to count on. He may be more clinging, cranky, anxious about your whereabouts, and fearful of strangers than usual even for this time of heightened dependence, or he may need to get back at you for your desertion. If you can handle your baby's "retribution," expressing his resentment will be good for him. Still noticeably wary about your whereabouts, he will eventually resume walking, but not until you have been back a while will he assume his usual spirit.

Disapproval from family or friends sways many mothers from their instinctive responses to their babies' pleas for extra support and physical contact. Try to remember that people have many reasons for doing things. Your husband's best friend may accuse you of spoiling the baby when you are not. Perhaps he envies the baby's ability to regress to an earlier dependency that he as an adult cannot assume. Perhaps an unmarried sister wishes that the baby might turn to her. Other members of the family may resent the baby's ability to monopolize your attention. Certainly the baby's brothers and sisters envy his ability to get what they are now too "grown-up" to ask for. Remember, too, that the baby is yours and your husband's. You understand him and your feelings best, so you are the best judge of your baby's needs. Even though you yourself might worry about spoiling him, *you* know down deep whether or not he has special needs at this time. This phase is common to babies in most of the world. It will pass once the baby is used to his new ability to separate from you and is able to incorporate it into his style of response. When he learns to do something about your absence, his anxiety will ebb. With support, your baby can reconsolidate his emotional resources to move toward greater autonomy.

One last thing to keep in mind is that babies who are unattached to their mothers are rarely very dependent on them. It is a compliment to you and your mothering that the baby trusts and cares for you.

Not only do babies with mothers sensitive and responsive to their needs and aware of their unique personalities have a physical, pleasurable, and comforting relationship with them, they also seem to be ahead in intellectual areas. They are much more able to conceptualize inanimate objects and people as permanent—a vital mental skill—with stable shapes and qualities whether or not they are out of sight and beyond contact.

Limits—Personal and Otherwise

The baby's fearfulness, which is limited to strange places and people, does not, of course, limit his explorations at home. His new physical and social freedom means that you must strike a balance between too much containment, which becomes oppression for the baby, and too much liberty, which can mean discomfort for the rest of the family or danger for the baby. Older children do need times when they are not saddled with the baby's constant presence and even mother needs some relief now and then.

The whole issue of containment, physical or social, is difficult for a baby and his parents. Discipline is all the harder now because the baby needs to exercise his brand-new "self-ness" and because he *is* more privileged. His daily "firsts" and accomplishments are toted out proudly.

Anger and punishment are often tough issues for parents to face honestly, especially if they have troubled memories of their own childhoods. Most adult responses, especially anger, are completely ineffective during a child's temper tantrum. Frequent punishment for errors can yield a sense of powerlessness that effectively stops learning.

Yet open anger at other times may not be "evil." A mother may be frightened by her now angry feelings, but punishment should not be coolly calculated. It will have no meaning to a baby. Too, a mother's incapacity to honestly respond to her baby may only encourage resistance to reasonable commands since the baby can have no clear sense of what his mother expects from him. The baby can understand an honest outbreak of anger, if you follow it by holding him and explaining that you are sorry about your anger, but you felt it was right, more easily than smoldering anger masked with cold patience. After all, very few of us can forget our own fright and anxiety as children when the air turned frigid with our own mothers' suppressed hostility. When a child has frequent tantrums—even twice a week is frequent —something may be wrong. Either he is running into a wall of "don'ts" or he has found that he can manipulate his parents. Sometimes the situation seems to involve no one but the baby. His budding attempts to sort "yes" from "no," "do" from "don't," "out" from "in," "down" from "up" create inner turmoil in him, too. Some babies have such a hard time with these decisions, especially when they are tired, that any mild rebuke or refusal may unleash a tempest of unapproachable screaming, head-banging and kicking. Reaching a child in the midst of a tantrum is very difficult.

Perhaps tantrums recall our own painful memories of ambivalence or impotence in making critical decisions. Screaming, slapping, or spanking the toddler are selfish ways to rid ourselves of our own bewilderment and tensions. They do not help the child. Waiting until your baby's hysteria has calmed and then comforting him with understanding and love are far better. While you are waiting, you can do a little self-examination to see what caused the tantrum and whether it could have been avoided. These responses are a distinct improvement over giving in to the baby's demands because you are afraid of his temper. Although it may not be apparent to you at first, your firmness will help the baby find his own personal controls and ultimately cut through the very indecision that drives him wild now. Developing these personal limits is crucial to your baby as he learns to move through the inner world of thought and feeling, just as recognition of physical limitations is necessary for learning to navigate the world of space and objects.

Motor

Large

Gets self to stand by flexing knees, pushing off from squat.
Standing, pivots body 90 degrees.
Walks, but still prefers crawling.
May add maneuvers to walking; e.g., stopping, waving, backing, carrying toys.
Climbs up and down stairs.
May climb out of crib or playpen.
Makes swimming movements in tub.

Sitting

Lowers self to sitting gracefully.

Small

Thumb apposition complete.

Takes covers off of containers.

Prefers one hand. Holds with one, maneuvers with the other.

Can point with index finger.
May push objects.

May undress self.

Language

Active

Controls intonation patterns.
Produces more sounds specific to native language of parent.

Aware of expressive function of language (e.g., repeats "damn" expectantly).

Practices words he knows.
Besides *Mama, Dada,* says two to eight words: possibly *no, baby, bye-bye, hi,* words that imitate sounds of objects, e.g., *bow-wow.*

Babbles short "sentences."

Passive

Words begin to assist in discrimination of object classes, *pei* is airplane and kite; i.e., flying objects.

Please do not regard this chart as a rigid timetable. Babies are unpredictable. Some perform an activity earlier or later than the chart indicates.

Growth Chart

Mental

Reaches accurately for something as he looks away.

Perceives objects as detached and separate, to be imitated, inserted into play routines, and related in time and space. Studies displacements of objects, rotates, reverses, and stacks things, places and removes them in and from containers; e.g., puts three or more blocks in cup; takes blocks and pellet out of box.

Unwraps toys. Finds toy under box, cup, pillow. Searches for hidden object even if he has not seen it hidden but only remembers where object was last seen. May search for it in more than one place.

Remembers events for longer and longer time.

Imitates a model more deliberately and precisely. Imitates behavior of an absent model.

Senses self as distinct from other things.
Uses and reaches with a preferred hand.
Uses one hand as holder, the other as explorer.

Through active trial and error, may find effective ways, truly new to him, to solve problems.

Differentiates personalities, trusts differentially.

Builds tower of two to three blocks after demonstration. Can group a few objects by shape and color. Likely to put one of two objects in mouth or under arm, grasps a third.

May mentally process actions or events before acting them out.

Social

Personal

Expresses many emotions and recognizes them in others.

Distinguishes self from others.

Interaction

Fears strange people and places. Reacts sharply to separation from mother.

Develops sense of humor.

Gives affection to humans and objects like toys and clothes. Negativism increases. Refuses eating a meal, new foods, mother's feeding; resists napping; may have tantrums.

Plays games with understanding. May give up toys upon request. Definitely prefers certain people to others.

Cultural

Usually insists on self-feeding.

Takes three meals a day. Holds cup to drink. Uses spoon. Plays with saucer.

May have trouble sleeping. One afternoon nap.

Cooperates in dressing.

Epilogue

Looking Back

It's been a long and exciting year, hasn't it? When you and your baby began your life together some twelve months ago, you were strangely new to each other. He was so very weak and helpless. All he could do was lie down. If you tried to sit him up, his gigantic head (with its "dangerous" soft spots) flopped every which way—so much so, you sometimes thought it might snap off his tender neck. If you touched him in certain spots, you triggered reflexes that came from every level of the evolutionary scale. The squeaks that emerged were unlike those of any language you had ever heard. He even looked funny. His skin was as wrinkled as an old man's, and he looked blue and water-logged. But the nurse kept telling you that this was *your* baby. Your pediatrician repeatedly assured you that all those weird twitches and spasms were perfectly normal, and had nothing to do with bad genes inherited from your great aunt on your mother's side, or the caudal anesthetic you took in your last hour of delivery.

After you won your first terrifying struggle to get your newborn to take the nipple and "please eat," he began to demand so much of you, you thought you'd weep from fatigue, and sometimes you really did. He ate and ate and ate. If you were a few minutes late, his piercing, insistent screams were enough to shatter your skull. The worst of it was that hunger, your first "explanation" for everything, wasn't always the problem. How desperately your mind raced over the countless details that could be wrong with him, and you matched them uselessly with the dicta of your mother and that bright young nurse from the hospital's mini-course on baby care. It took you weeks to realize that you had to come up with your own solutions, that sometimes your baby cried because he was as frustrated as you were with his inability to reach out and get into that world that was going on above his prone and clumsy little body.

All that you *were* sure of was that ferociously strong, some-how reassuring grip on your finger from an incredibly tiny fist; the jerky, valiant efforts of a wobbling head to turn toward you; and the intense, momentary gaze from eyes still bruised from the battle of birth and its aftermath. Even then, how could you be certain of anything in the hospital when you had him only those precious few minutes after feedings? Still, he seemed to be picking up some echoes from an environment totally alien to the warm, safe womb he had been at home in. These things (not the "love" the baby books preached) guided you and so did your sense that somehow you mattered to him and you had to help because no one else cared as much.

And here he is now, just a year later. He can sit anywhere, stand, stoop, climb, and probably walk. Next thing you know, he'll be running. He can reach out for things, grab them with a favorite hand, and search for something lost. He can say a few words and he can understand you! He smiles at you, throws back his head and laughs with you, hugs you, gets angry at you, and weeps if you go away. He is such a lovable creature he even extends his affection to a brother or sister and to his grandparents, although he can be pretty cool toward strangers. Instead of the chaos of 3 A.M. feedings and unexplainable crying, he eats and sleeps at pretty much the same times you do now. What is more, he likes it that way. He relishes certain tastes and smells and detests others. He wants to listen to, look into and manipulate *everything*. He can attend closely to a block tower he is building *and* listen carefully for the sounds at the front door signaling father's homecoming! He can deliberately empty all your pots and pans from the kitchen cabinets merely to solve the problem of how to get them all back in again. Though such relentless curiosity can be totally exasperating at times, his sheer, exuberant joy in learning and discovering as simple a thing as his face in a mirror delights you and your husband constantly. Most of all, he has become a person among others. He is somewhat aware of this too, because he can remember people, places, events, and things, and he senses that they have substance independent of his.

Can you believe it? You have come so far together in such a short, whirlwind time. He was born only a breath ago. Together you have learned to navigate the worlds of people, space, and thought. Now that he has begun to get around physically, your toddler will practice upright balancing and master the techniques of handling himself physically in more and more situations. His world, enlarged beyond mother and father, requires communication with people less tuned in to his signals and silent cues. So he has a purpose and readiness for mastering words and learning the grammar of his language. Having begun a career of reciprocation and exchange with you and the immediate family, your child is ready to use his language, his culture and his mind to chart his own special course in the world beyond infancy.

Some Books for Parents

THE CHILDREN OF THE DREAM by Bruno Bettelheim, Macmillan, 1969.
A treatment of the growth and development of infants and preschoolers in the group-care projects of Israel.

INFANTS AND MOTHERS: DIFFERENCES IN DEVELOPMENT by T. Berry Brazelton, M.D., Delacorte Press, 1971.
An authoritative guide for new parents. Reviews the health habits and emotional development of an active, passive, and normal infant in the first twelve months of life.

THE POWER OF PLAY by Frank and Theresa Caplan, Doubleday & Co., 1973.
Examines the power of play, fantasy, and toys as they affect the personality, social, body, and cognitive growth of infants, toddlers and preschoolers.

YOUR CHILD, KEEPING HIM HEALTHY by Child Health Centers of America, Inc., 1972.
A simply written health manual prepared by pediatricians to answer parents' common questions on physical growth, diseases, safety, nutrition, and other problems of infants, toddlers, and preschoolers. Includes record-keeping charts on immunizations, weight and height, visits to doctor.

THE MAGIC YEARS by Selma Fraiberg, Charles Scribner & Sons, 1959.
A top psychoanalyst discusses how children mature from birth to six years of age, and some theories and facts about feeding, talking, sex education, fantasy, self-control, fear, and other subjects in practical terms.

BABY LEARNING THROUGH BABY PLAY by Ira J. Gordon, Ph.D., St. Martin's Press, 1971.
A guide to a new parent's job as teacher. Describes songs, games, and physical activities to promote interpersonal relations and early language.

CHILD BEHAVIOR by Frances L. Ilg, M.D. and Louise Bates Ames, Ph.D., Harper and Row, 1966.
Two child development experts review physical and behavior problems of early childhood. Specific advice on eating, fears, sex development, relationships with children and parents, discipline, etc.

WHAT EVERY CHILD WANTS HIS PARENTS TO KNOW by Lee Salk, Ph.D., McKay, 1972.
All the questions asked by new parents about child health and behavior are answered by this leading pediatric psychologist of New York Hospital.

BABY AND CHILD CARE by Benjamin Spock, MD., Pocketbook Division of Simon and Shuster, 1968.
A popular standard reference for health and child development problems of infants and preschoolers.

THE U.S. GOVERNMENT BOOK OF INFANT CARE, U.S. Department of Health, Education and Welfare, Office of Child Development, Universal Publishing Company, 1968.
A revised updated edition of standard government publication on the care of an infant in the first year of life.

Index

THE PRINCETON CENTER FOR INFANCY AND EARLY CHILDHOOD is a pioneering research, development and publishing organization. It was established by many members of the same team that founded and built Creative Playthings, Inc., and is headed by Frank Caplan, its former president. The Center is involved with professional and government organizations preparing films, pamphlets and parent educational materials. Mr. Caplan has also co-authored, with his wife, a book entitled *The Power of Play*.